Learning to Pray

Learning to Pray

Lessons from the Masters

Edited by
Peter Lemass

Veritas Publications Dublin 1977

First published 1977 by
Veritas Publications
Veritas House, 7/8 Lower Abbey Street, Dublin 1

© 1977 Peter Lemass

Set in 10 pt Journal Roman and printed
and bound in the Republic of Ireland by
Cahill (1976) Limited, Dublin

Designed by Liam Miller
Cover by Steven Hope

NIHIL OBSTAT:
Richard Sherry, DD

IMPRIMI POTEST:
✠Dermot,
Archbishop of Dublin.
June 1977.

ISBN 0 905092 35 X
Cat. No. 3356

Contents

1   St Augustine

His life, times and spirituality

In terms of history more than fifteen hundred years separate us from Augustine. We live in a world which despite certain superficial similarities with his age is a totally different world from his. Ours is predominantly a time of rapid change, so rapid in fact that the achievements, chiefly scientific, of the modern era have eclipsed almost at one go what the combined weight of previous centuries took to achieve. The trite phrase "man has come of age" is used to signify the fundamental difference between the man of today and the man of the late fourth and early fifth centuries—Augustine's era. We are told that man is at long last his own master. There seems to be no limit to his possibilities. But has man himself changed out of all recognition?

Andrew Greely points out in his book *The persistence of religion*[1] that man's basic needs, his religious needs, have not changed. On the contrary they have become more acute and baffling than ever. There appears to be no meaning to life, no ultimate goal. The question posed by the psalmist still remains: "What is man?" (Psalm 8:5). The influential English writer F. R. Leavis said recently: "Humanity's sickness is that it has nothing to believe in . . . people cannot live without a sense of significance."[2]

The need for meaning to life is matched in the modern world by a desire for transcendence. The secularisers have done their work. They have encouraged man to live for himself, to suck out all he can from his environment, to live his own life according to his own convenience, and to regulate—if that be the right phrase—his conduct, not in the light of any moral code, but simply in accordance with what the law of the land prescribes or allows. A modern Russian poet, Yevtushenko, a convinced Marxist, wrote in the *Guardian* (one of the most influential English dailies) on 23 December 1975: "What will save nature and man? . . . Mankind is now, as never before, in need of great philosophers. . . Man can expect help from no one else but himself. If today he is drowning in a whirlpool of problems, only he can drag himself out by the hair." What a bleak prospect!

The short answer to the central problem of the meaning of man which Augustine offers is the celebrated dictum found in the opening chapter of his *Confessions*: "Fecisti nos ad te!" God made us for himself and our hearts are restless until they rest in him. There is a world of meaning in this one sentence, which might be said to sum up Augustine's whole philosophy of man. We did not make ourselves. God made us, and it is in him alone that the problem of human existence finds its solution. In short, as Charles Boyer notes,[3] the ultimate meaning and purpose of life according to Augustine is the possession of God. This is the highest and most enduring form of happiness. Only God can fully satisfy the human heart.

It may be claimed that few if any Christian writers, or for that matter non-Christian writers, ever plumbed the depths of the human heart as did Augustine. A modern psychiatrist has not hesitated to say in print that Augustine's *Confessions* is "perhaps the most profound psychological analysis ever carried out."[4] What invests Augustine's thought with a truly contemporary relevance is that, as Gilson puts it, "each of us has his Augustinian moments, his Augustinian moods."[5]

Augustine experienced in its most acute form the desire of man for the truth about himself, and the answer to his insatiable longing for happiness or fulfilment. Augustine's struggles, weaknesses, false starts, errors, above all his humanity and passionate feeling, may find an echo in all of us. Though he was a man of real genius, of unsurpassed originality and profundity of thought, Augustine was one with the common man. He did not derive his knowledge and understanding of humanity, of what makes a man tick, from Aristotle's *Ethics* or from other writers but from his own personal experience. One can sense, almost feel, this in his writings, especially his incomparable *Confessions*.

Augustine's approach to the problem of man is in a remarkable degree truly existential. I think the special relevance of his spirituality lies here. Man in the concrete, the *I*, the *whole* man, is the problem to which he addresses himself. On the basis of experience and revelation he constructed not a system but a philosophy of man as well as a theology of God and society, captivated as he advanced by the beauty of nature, of all of God's creation of which man is the masterpiece, but above all by the truth, the goodness and beauty of the creator: "O Beauty, ever ancient, ever new, late have I known you, late have I loved you" — but fortunately for himself and for us, too, not too late!

Before attempting to delineate some of the basic principles and themes of Augustine's spirituality with reference to our time, I must sound two warnings. Much of what I have to say will be familiar to you already, not only because of your own reading of Augustine but because our Christian tradition is impregnated with his thought. After St Paul, Augustine was the greatest single formative influence on Christian thought and piety. Secondly, Augustine's view of the spiritual life is an intensely personal one. In order to understand it, one must try to see it in its historical context.

We shall derive a misleading impression, indeed we shall almost inevitably give a wrong slant to his teaching, if we isolate Augustine from his milieu, and if we ignore his highly individualistic approach and temperament, and close our eyes to his inadequacies. He himself was the first to admit them. As always we have to work out for ourselves the solution to our own personal problems, but Augustine points if not the way, at least where the solution must ultimately be found. Pope Celestine I, who sent to Ireland its first bishop in the person of Palladius, described Augustine shortly after his death on 28 August 430 as one of the greatest masters of the Church: "Inter magistros optimos."[6] Augustine is still the master.

Augustine like so many young people today yearned to be self-sufficient, to understand himself and to find and possess the truth or wisdom which is happiness. He rejected his mother's religion, the authority of the catholic Church, because in his view it was a religion based on credulity and superstition. Instead he enrolled in the sect of the Manichees, who vaunted their religion as the religion of the intelligentsia. Nothing was to be accepted unless it could be proved by reason. Moreover, the Manichees claimed to have a rational explanation of the problem of evil, a question that had the deepest personal interest for Augustine. The surprising thing is that a man of Augustine's intelligence and honesty remained a member of the sect for nine years. The system was a fraud, and when Augustine finally broke away he took refuge in scepticism. He was on the brink of despair.

There is no need to elaborate here on Augustine's painful odyssey in search of the truth; how he discovered the radical insufficiency of man's unaided powers of intellect and will to find the truth which satisfies not only the mind but also fulfils the desire of the human heart, its capacity and yearning for the immutable and the infinite which God has implanted in all men. If Augustine sometimes appears to underestimate or downgrade the resources of human nature, it is simply because he was convinced from his own personal history of one's inablity without the light of faith and the liberating power of grace to satisfy the desires of the mind and heart.

The important thing is that he did find, although it took

him some twenty years, the answer to the problem of the meaning of life, and it is encouraging for us that he emphasises the ability of every man to discover the truth for himself. Augustine was anything but an elitist. He argued that there must be a universal way, one open to all; that contemplation is not the preserve of the few; that the power to achieve supreme happiness is available to anyone who humbly seeks the truth and is of good will.

This was one point which Augustine stoutly maintained against the neo-platonists, however much he admired their philosophy. They held that the ascent to the One and the possession of wisdom was the reserve of the few. Augustine on the contrary showed that Christ by becoming incarnate not only opened the way to everyone—he is in fact the way —but in addition he offers the power which we need in order to attain the wisdom of God which is happiness.[7] This he did as the one mediator between God and man; mediator *in quantum homo* and as such accessible to all.[8] God first loved us and became man out of pure love for men. He came to restore human nature to its original perfection; but in his infinite goodness he did something much more than that. He elevated human nature, raising it to an immeasurably higher state, to a participation in the divine nature itself: in a word transcendence or deification.[9] This dazzling prospect will remain unattainable as long as we continue to regard ourselves as self-sufficient.

Augustine's spirituality, which has its roots deep in a profound understanding of human nature and above all in God's word, revolves around two poles: the one self-knowledge, the other love, or to be more precise, self-knowledge and knowledge of God, and self-love and love of God.[10] We can only make the truth our own if we are willing to subject our intellect to the guidance of faith and our will to the movements of grace. No one, says Augustine, can believe unless he is willing to believe.[11] But this is exactly where the problem of modern man lies, that is the self-sufficient man. It is not so much that he is intellectually arrogant, but rather that the will to believe is lacking or, to put it another way, man lacks the specifically Christian attitude of humility which Augustine calls the sign of Christ.[12] He knew from the inside the barrier which pride in one's intellectual ability erects between God and man. And so, difficult as it was for him, he made humility the foundation of his spiritual life. The higher one wishes to ascend, the deeper one must descend.[13]

This brings us face to face with one of the greatest problems confronting the world today. Erich Fromm has stated that "love is the only sane and satisfactory answer to the problem of human existence".[14] But without humility one cannot even begin to love. Fromm adds, possibly with some exaggeration, that humility is such a rare virtue that few achieve the capacity to love. He asks the pointed question: How many truly loving persons do you know?

Augustine firmly bases the acquisition of humility on self-knowledge and knowledge of God. For him the shortest and most perfect prayer in the early days of his conversion was: "God always the same, may I know myself, may I know you."[15] We are all familiar with, perhaps even bored by, the so-called crisis of identity. The fact is, however, that it is essential that I know myself and understand myself before I can hope to know and love anyone else. Augustine's spirituality for all its simplicity is one of depth. It means asking telling questions, for example, Who am I? Each of us has a mental picture of himself, a sort of image, but does it correspond with reality, with the real *I*? If we do not know ourselves we cannot love ourselves, and if we cannot love ourselves, what hope have we of loving our neighbour as we love ourselves? "Men can speak," says Augustine, "they can see... they can hear; but who can penetrate one's thought, who can inspect one's heart?" And he goes on to point out that there are depths in man of which man himself is ignorant.[16]

If we descend into the innermost part of self we discover

something of vital importance for the spiritual life. We realise that our real self, the soul, is made in the image and likeness of God; that we have received our real being neither from ourselves nor from anybody else but from God. We are because he made us. This realisation is the beginning of the truth about ourselves. It is the bedrock of humility. But this knowledge, far from being petrifying or debasing, reveals how exalted man's nature is. It is *capax divini*. This is no mere poetical conclusion. It underlines something that is too often overlooked or ignored, namely that every human being, every person, is a singular creation on the part of God and as such is worthy of not only the deepest respect but of our love. In Augustine's spirituality the unity of the human race and the equality of all men because of their common origin, which derives ultimately from God's goodness, looms large; but basically what moves Augustine to admiration and wonder is the individual, the soul of each man which God fashions according to his own image and likeness.

Nothing is more intimate to a man than his soul, for it is his spirit. The powers of the soul, latent as they may be, are ontologically immense. A man can know through the power of intelligence which is a participation of God's intelligence and knowledge of himself. A man can love in virtue of his will which is a participation of God's will. A man has memory or consciousness of himself, his separateness, identity, personality. His consciousness or *memoria sui* is a participation of God's consciousness of himself. Man's soul, which is God's image, was grossly disfigured by the Fall, however. The restoration of that image is one of the essential processes of the spiritual life, and can only be effected by grace. For Augustine it amounts in effect to a new creation. Transformed by grace, the soul begins to enjoy a union with God in which the relationship between creator and creature is subsumed in a relationship of lovers. This union of love is summed up by Augustine in a typically

daring sentence but one which harmonises perfectly with
his characteristic understanding of the effect of love. "By
loving God," he says, "we become gods!"[17]

Here it should be pointed out in passing that although
the union between the soul and God, according to Augustine, is achieved through charity, the greatest of the theological virtues, none the less faith and hope have a vital role.
Faith purifies the intellect and thus enables the soul to see
God, however obscurely.[18] Hope strengthens the memory
or the soul's consciousness by assuring it of God's goodness,
mercy and promises. But it is charity which moves the will
to love God with joy and fervour. Harking back, however,
to his basic theme, the interaction of knowledge and love,
Augustine writes:

> If we wish to love God, we must know God. If a
> man must love his neighbour as himself, he must
> first love himself by loving God. But how can he do
> this if he does not know God, if he does not know
> himself?[19]

Evidently the acquistion of self-knowledge and knowledge of God is not an end in itself. It is only a means,
essential no doubt, towards the development of love. On
the other hand Augustine insists, and in doing so started a
tradition which medieval spiritual writers and mystics, for
example St Catherine of Siena, inherited, namely that the
more we know God, the more we love him, and the more
we love him, the more we know him.[20] Yet love or charity
is the inspiration and goal of Augustine's whole teaching on
the spiritual life. Long before he read in St John that God
is charity his one wish was to love and be loved. In the
autumn of 370 he arrived in Carthage to study at what one
may loosely call the university. He tells us what his feelings
were:

> I came to Carthage... I was not yet in love, but I
> was in love with love, and from the very depth of

> my need hated myself for not more keenly feeling
> the need. I sought some object to love. . . I hated
> security [how modern!] and a life with no snares
> for my feet. . . My longing then was to love and be
> loved, but most when I obtained the enjoyment of
> the body of the person who loved me.[21]

Augustine frankly admits that before his conversion he
could not live without a woman, but he was not a libertine.
Indeed it is doubtful if he found more satisfaction in extra-
marital sex than he did in the company of male friends. In
his *Confessions* he has penned probably the most moving
account ever written of the joy of human friendship. Speaking of his friends he says:

> All kinds of things rejoiced my soul in their company
> —to talk and laugh and do each other kindnesses;
> read pleasant books together, pass from lightest jest-
> ing to talk of the deepest things; differ without
> rancour, as a man might differ with himself, and
> when most rarely dissension arose find our normal
> agreement all the sweeter for it; teach each other to
> learn from each other; be impatient for the return
> of the absent, and welcome them with joy on their
> homecoming; these and such like things, proceeding
> from our hearts as we gave affection and received it
> back, and shown by face, by voice, by the eyes, and
> a thousand other pleasing ways, kindled a flame
> which fused our very souls and of many made one.
>
> This is what men value in friends, and value so much
> that their conscience judges them guilty if they do
> not meet friendship with friendship, expecting
> nothing from their friend save such evidence of his
> affection.[22]

Elsewhere Augustine wrote that life is bitter and hard and
loses all its joy and colour if we have no friends: "Whenever
a man is without a friend, not a single thing in the world
appears friendly to him."[23] But Augustine also reminds us
that there is only one way to keep friends and to be re-

assured when they die:

> Blessed is the man that loves thee, O God, and his friend in thee, and his enemy in thee. For he alone loses no one that is dear to him, if all are dear in God, who is never lost. And who is that God but our God, the God who made heaven and earth?

A man has no choice but to love. "If you love nothing." says Augustine, "you will be lazy, lifeless, detestable, miserable."[24] And yet for all the talk, commercialisation, of love which distinguishes our age, the fact remains that, according to a leading modern psychologist, "love is a marginal phenomenon in present-day Western society."[25] He gives two reasons. Man is treated as a commodity, and the "negation of love of man has gone hand in hand with rejection of the love of God."

This is an arresting observation, particularly as its author refuses to accept God as a person and denies the historicity of the Incarnation as well. I may make bold to suggest that Augustine would rewrite Professor Fromm's statement to read: "The negation of love of man has gone hand in hand with rejection of the love of God precisely because of man's refusal to love God." If we do not love God, we do not love at all, simply because we do not know what love is or, as Augustine would put it, we do not love love![26] Why? Because God is love. He loved us before we could ever love him.[27] We do not give ourselves either love or the power to love. We have this priceless gift, no doubt, but it is God's gift to us.

Love has many meanings. Augustine reduces all love to two kinds: love of ourselves (*amor sui*) and love of God (*amor dei*).[28] When we speak of self-love we have to make a crucial distinction. What Augustine means by love of self, which amounts to contempt of God, is selfishness, and he demonstrates that this attitude is paradoxically hatred of oneself. It is therefore something inhuman. Augustine, even if he were not gifted, as he was, with an extraordinary capacity for friendship and love of people, would have been flying in the face of Scripture if he were to deny the immense value and beauty of human love, of the love of man for man. The love of man for man or a feeling of humanity is more fundamental than any kind of human love, even the love which a father has for his son.[29]

On the other hand, if it is a virtue, an inescapable demand on the part of God, that I must love my neighbour —every man, because he is a human being—surely it must be a virtue by the same token to love myself, since I am a human being too. It is wrong to regard love of self and love of one's neighbour as two alternatives; to assume that the more I love myself, the less I love or can love others. If I cannot love myself, I cannot love anyone else.[30] Selfishness, the *amor sui* which Augustine classifies as amounting to contempt of God, not to speak of man, is quite another matter. It is not love but cupidity. Selfishness in fact is only another name for narcissism, a state which makes one incapable of loving.

The problem is not whether one should love, but how and what we should love. "Purify your love," urges Augustine, "rechannel into the garden the water flowing into the sewer."[31] For him the problem of love is basically a problem of liberation. We cannot properly direct our love unless we have the power to do so. It is not a question of being able to choose what to love, but to love within the meaning of the word, that is to give ourselves to others, not for any selfish motive, but purely out of love.

This raised for Augustine the whole question of liberty and grace. We are living in an age which might be called among other things the age of neo-pelagianism. The British monk, Pelagius, had the most wonderful faith in unaided human nature. He held, for instance, that man's will was not affected by the Fall, and hence we do not need grace in order to live rightly, which means in effect to love rightly. Augustine rebelled against pelagianism because it contra-

dicted his own experience of himself—here he speaks for
most if not all of us!—and because it ran counter to Romans
7:19-25. From the moment that he read this text of St Paul
Augustine attributed everything to grace. In short, man can
only do what God gives him the power to do, namely to
love God with his whole heart and soul, and his neighbour
as himself. Hence Augustine's classic prayer: "Give what
you command and command what you will."[32]

There is no need for me to emphasise how relevant
Augustine's teaching on this subject is today, perhaps even
more so today than in the fifth century. Modern man
glories in his self-sufficiency and power. The humanist
glories in his own goodness. Grace is a free gift on the part
of God independently of any merit of ours. As grace
develops and works within us, selfishness diminishes and
concurrently our capacity for loving others increases.
Augustine indeed identifies grace with charity. Moreover,
when we cooperate with God's gift we begin to experience
a delight in loving beyond and above ourselves. No one can
love unless he wills to love, but our will needs grace in order
to be effective.

Augustine, then, attributes love to God who makes our
will good by his grace, and continues to help it to be good
and to do good; in a word to love in the true sense.[33] Even
so, God does not take over, as it were. It is your will that
must do the loving. We do not love with our lips, our hands
or our bodies. When one writes a letter, says Augustine, it is
the heart which writes: the hand only makes visible what is
in the heart. If we do not love with and from the heart or
the will we are guilty of deception. Our nearness to or
remoteness from both God and our fellow man depends on
the quality and intensity of our love.

In his commentary on the first letter of St John, Augustine reveals the whole bent of his thought by declaring that
he could never satisfy himself when speaking about charity.
At the same time he does insist that there must be order in

our love. We need to evaluate things at their proper worth. This is absolutely necessary where love is concerned.

Augustine was anything but a kill-joy. In one of his sermons he read the mind of his audience. "You desire life and happiness," he said. Very well: "far from curbing your desire I stimulate it all the more."[34] "God does not forbid you to love the things of this world. . . [how could he?] he gave you all these things. Therefore love him as their maker. He wants to give you more, himself no less. If you love these things and neglect God who created them, what sort of love do you think this should be called?"[35] A man is as his love is. "Do you love the earth? You will be earth. Do you love God? What shall I say? You will be God."[36]

Our first love, therefore, must be God. He has every right not merely to our love, but to all our love. Indeed we must love him not just as we love ourselves; we must love him more than ourselves, even more than our parents. Augustine points out in rather homely fashion that although we are their children, they did not make us. When they made love to each other they had no idea who, if anyone, would be born. God knew, for it was he who gave us life.[37] Rightly then "does he demand the whole of you"— all your love—"he who made you."[38] He does so simply in order to fill you with himself, who is perfect happinesss, so that in this way you can find yourself and fulfil yourself. When we love God we really love ourselves. Indeed, "only the man who loves God knows how to love himself."[39]

Augustine's philosophy of love is therefore one of transcendence. The acid test of our love of God, however, is love of our neighbour. The two stand or fall together, because it is the same love with which we love God and our neighbour,[40] since love of its nature is indivisible.[41] Augustine with unerring instinct, which his reading of Scripture amply confirmed, made charity the supreme law of the Christian life, and in particular of Augustinian monasticism. It is the *ante omnia* as the rule intones.

In an Augustinian monastery everything is centred on charity. "If something is opposed to charity it is scrapped and done away with; if something offends against charity it is not allowed to last one day. Charity is so commanded by Christ and the apostles that if this one thing be lacking all else is useless; if charity is present all things are fulfilled."[42] Taking his stand on Romans 13:10 Augustine justifies his forthright attitude by asking: "What can be lacking where there is charity? What is there that can be of use if charity is missing?"[43]

Augustine would subscribe whole-heartedly, but with greater precision, to Erich Fromm's statement that brotherly love is "the most fundamental kind of love."[44] Scripture tells us that we must love God before all else. This is the first and greatest commandment. But Christ coupled with it, as a necessary corollary, the commandment to love our neighbour as ourself. So close is the nexus between the two that Augustine seems to have been in two minds as to which commandment constituted perfection. At a comparatively early stage in his theological development he had no doubt that man's perfection consists solely in the love of God.[45] But he could not decide how the perfection of charity was to be achieved. He inclined to the view that the process begins with our loving God, but that it is perfected by loving one's neighbour.

Later he made a distinction, God is one thing, he said in a sermon, the neighbour is another. No doubt they are loved with one and the selfsame charity, but they are not one. We are commanded to love God first and then our neighbour. But, he added, "one begins with the second in order to arrive at the first."[46] If we do not love our brother whom we see, how can we love God whom we do not see? Augustine, however, was absolutely sure on one point: "There is no surer step towards the love of God. . . than the love of man for man." It is easier, he adds, to do lesser things than greater things.

A marked change of emphasis with regard to the perfection of charity is discernible in *On the Trinity*, Augustine's greatest theological work, which was sixteen years in the making (c. 400-416). In Book VIII he states that the love of one's neighbour would appear to be the only requisite for perfection; indeed he declares that St John emphatically identified brotherly love with perfection.[47] Nonetheless Augustine points out that the two commandments, to love God and to love our neighbour, come to the same thing.[48] We cannot love our neighbour unless we love God, and we cannot love God unless we love our neighbour. There is this difference, however, and it is a crucial one. We love God for himself, that is as an end in himself; we love ourselves and our neighbour, not as ends in themselves but for God.[49]

It goes without saying that God's love for man is on an entirely different plane from man's love for man. The fact of the matter is that there is absolutely no equality whatever between God and man. His love for us is infinitely greater than our love for him can ever be. With our neighbour it is otherwise. Here there is equality, not that all men are the same but that all are one. If I have developed the capacity for loving, I cannot but help loving my brother. There is of course a difference between loving another person and loving him as I love myself. The gap was bridged by Christ when he became man. He perfected natural love and gave it a new dimension. He transformed our capacity for love and showed what human love can be at its finest, that is when purified and elevated and expanded by grace. In short, Christ enabled us, if we will, to love each other, not just as we love ourselves but as he loved us.

It is only when our love is perfect that we can say with Augustine "love and do as you will".[50] This robust phrase, which might stand as the motto of modern youth, is not an invitation to "free" love. What Augustine means is that whatever we do, we should do it out of love. If you are silent, be silent out of love; if you speak, speak out of love;

if you correct, correct out of love; if you spare, spare out of love.[51] The phrase covers a multitude, as does charity. If we love our neighbour we will do all we can to help him to love God. There is no higher form of charity either to ourselves or to others.

Augustine's vision extended beyond the relationship between man and man to the unity between all peoples, regardless of race, colour or nationality. God planned the unity of the human race from the beginning when he formed one single man, says Augustine, from whom all others descend. Polygenesis doubtless appears to provide a satisfactory explanation for the origin of the diversity of peoples, but apart from its theological implications it takes from the physical unity of the human race which Augustine manfully sought to underline. In his view all men are one through Adam, apart altogether from their unity in Christ. Through our common ancestor we are all physically and not merely morally one family.

Augustine's message to the world at large is that God destined the peoples of the world to form one society based on nature and united by charity. Every event in the history of man, no matter how disconcerting; every person, even the humblest, the handicapped, the mentally defective finds his justification in the City of God. Through and in Jesus Christ all the baptised and potentially all non-Christians form the new people of God. They are no longer Jew or Greek or whatever, but one in Chirst. There is no room for racism in Augustine's *Weltanschauung*. He was in fact strongly anti-racist. Men are men whatever else they may be.

Augustine does not identify the city of God with the catholic Church. The city includes all the predestined and only the predestined. Nevertheless, he points out that the city of God on earth is essentially the catholic Church. His ideal of one world demands that there be one God and one Church. To attempt, as the humanist aims, to build a better world, a universal brotherhood without Christ is doomed to failure. It is Christ's will and promise that all would be one. To fulfil his will and realise his promise is impossible without him. "If we really want one world," says Gilson, commenting on Augustine's *On the city of God*, "we must first have one Church, and the only Church that is one is the Catholic Church." This is the only viable and valid basis on which men may hope to construct Augustine's plan of a universal society, the city of God on earth, united by nature, faith, hope and charity. As Christians we have among other things the duty of promoting the unity of God's people, and this we shall best do by being ourselves living examples of that first Christian community whose spirit of one mind and one heart turned to God Augustine embodied in his rule. The final word rightly belongs to Henri Marrou:

> The greatest temptation humanity has to face in the course of its pilgrimage through the ages is to forget —fascinated as we are by the genuinely real splendour of strictly earthly goods—to forget the supreme glory of God, and that he is the goal, the End of the journey. . . It is well that all should remind themselves that man is not in the world for himself, nor yet for the world, but for God, that man is not just an animal species whose function is to build civilisations, like ants and termites endlessly labouring to build and rebuild their wonderful but fragile dwellings. It is good, it is wholesome, to be put in mind that by means of all these temporary scaffoldings which are men's works the divine Architect is building up the City of God, the one lasting home where man may know eternal rest.[52]

Augustine and prayer

No subject of a spiritual nature with the sole exception of Scripture has perhaps evoked more interest in recent times than prayer. This is all to the good. It is not an exaggeration to hold that never before in the history of Christianity was prayer more necessary than today. We are living in a world that has become increasingly secularised with a consequent loss of a sense of the transcendent, accompanied by a pernicious view of man's autonomy. Augustine's teaching on prayer provides for one thing a corrective, an antidote to the malaise that threatens to engulf us. On any reckoning he was one of the greatest masters and practitioners of prayer. His understanding of prayer is all the more relevant because of some strange theories which have been propounded and doubtless will continue to be advanced in our own day.

For example, the excellent English Jesuit journal of spirituality, *The Way*, carried an article early in 1976 in which the author set out to "rationalise" and "demystify" the meaning of prayer.[1] The idea that prayer is an encounter or dialogue with God is rejected; indeed we are told that "God cannot be directly addressed by man in prayer"! The author's notion of petitionary prayer is extremely curious. It certainly is not Augustinian.

It is impossible in the course of a single essay to deal at all adequately with Augustine's teaching on prayer. He never composed a formal treatise on the subject,[2] although his philosophy of man and his vast theological output contain such an enormous wealth of insights into and reflections on prayer that one is confronted with a veritable *embarras*

24

de richesses. Augustine's inability to organise his thoughts and follow a systematic pattern, or pursue a line of thought right through to the end, as always presents a problem. No one study of his teaching on prayer can hope to be complete or do anything like justice to the man whose profundity of thought and richness of mind have rarely if ever been matched in the history of Christian spirituality.[3]

For Augustine prayer is essentially a question of desire.[4] As such it is an expression of man's deepest aspiration—the desire for happiness, not any kind of happiness but happiness which is total, lasting and perfect. Many people, perhaps the majority, may be content with a measure of happiness and settle for a state of peaceful coexistence with themselves and others. There are people, young people in particular, who seek happiness in terms of self-control or mastery over the mind and body, if not indeed ecstasy. They yearn for an inner experience of the transcendent. In Zen it is called illumination. Some have actually travelled to the Far East in order to be instructed by a guru in the practice of transcendental meditation. Once upon a time wise men came west following the guiding star. Now it would appear to be the other way round!

Practitioners of transcendental meditation adamantly insist that their technique is not simply a kind of prayer but is *the* prayer. It might be interesting, and maybe profitable, to compare Augustine's teaching on the ascent of the soul to or its search for God and union with Wisdom itself, which is beatifying, with the transcendental method. There is, however, a fundamental difference between Augustine's basic assumptions and approach, to say no more, and the teaching of Zen. According to Augustine all prayer is God's gift in the first place, which is another way of saying that all prayer is infused. No doubt the desire of happiness expresses a longing which is essentially natural, but the impulse to pray as well as the will and power to pray come from God.

In one of his sermons Augustine puts himself in the place of the man who regards prayer as primarily a human activity, even though faith enters in. "I prayed that he [God] might give me something," says Augustine, impersonating this kind of man, "and in order to pray I believed beforehand. I gave myself faith, and God gave me what in my belief I prayed for." "I can see you saying this, " replies Augustine, "that you first gave something to God that he might give you the rest." Augustine quotes Romans 11:34-5 and comments: "Did you first give something to God which he did not give you? Where did you get it, you a beggarman? What have you that you have not received? You give to God what is God's; he receives from you what he gave you."[5]

Without the gift of faith it is impossible to pray. This faith is not just intellectual belief but the faith that works through charity and includes hope as an indispensable corollary. In effect Augustine's teaching on prayer is bound up with his theology of grace. Writing to the future Pope Sixtus III (432-440), he points out that although God gives faith to the man who does not pray, nonetheless man could not pray at all unless God granted him that gift in the first place, for it is faith that prays.[6] The exercise of transcendental meditation may be psychologically satisfying, even beneficial, but from the Christian point of view it can only be described in Augustine's phrase as "great strides but off the track".[7] If faith is wanting, prayer ceases, since prayer is itself an exercise of faith. On the other hand it goes without saying that if we have no hope we will not pray, and without charity we do not pray as Christ taught us how to pray. Only the person who loves God and his neighbour prays in and through the Spirit by whom the love of God is poured forth in our hearts. Prayer is God's mercy to us, and it is a sobering thought, as Augustine reminds us, that if we do not pray we have no hope of forgiveness.[8]

If prayer is a gift from God, given without any antecedent merit on our part, which is the authentic teaching of

Augustine, it follows that the will and what is equally necessary the power to pray depend on God's grace. Only *NB* the humble receive it because only the humble ask for it, granted that God can and does grant his grace on occasion without our asking for it, provided we are ready to accept his gift. God uses our felt need of something—mercy, forgiveness, consolation, help, in a word our sense of insufficiency—in order to draw us to himself; to intensify our desire so that ultimately what the transcendentalists aspire to may be ours in an infinitely deeper, more perfect degree, namely union with God himself who is the end of all our desires and is happiness itself, supreme, immutable, eternal.

The gift of prayer is one thing; the use of the gift is something else. There is no room for quietism in Augustine's theory of prayer. When God gives grace he does not take over as it were and deprive the will of its proper activity. On the contrary, the effect of grace is to assist the will of man to do what of itself it is powerless or too weak to do. Scripture no doubt says that the Spirit himself intercedes for us. Augustine explains this problematical statement of St Paul (Romans 8:26)—we may ask how can the Spirit be said to pray to God?—by stating that the Spirit prompts us to pray by inspiring in us the desire, and assists us at the same time in praying.[9] Yet it is the heart which prays, that is the mind, will and memory, in other words the soul. For Augustine the soul of man is always the focus of prayer. Hence interiorism is the pivot of Augustinian prayer, as it is of Augustinian spirituality as a whole.

Interiorism means first of all returning into oneself. In a way it is like the return of the prodigal son. After wandering abroad for quite some time and having wasted his substance seeking happiness where it was not to be found, that is outside himself, the young man "entered into himself", says the gospel. This introversion was the start of his conversion, his return to his father. The process is described by Augustine in terms of descending or returning into one's deepest self and of transcending oneself: "Do not go out-side; return into yourself. Truth dwells in the interior man; and if you find that your nature is mutable, transcend your-self."[10]

Prayer in depth is about the soul and God. It is seeking the truth about oneself and God: *noverim me, noverim te!* The truth is to be found deep within the recesses of my soul, for it is there that Christ dwells.[11] In his *Confessions* Augustine describes how in his manichean days he longed for the truth:

> O my supreme and good Father, Beauty of all things beautiful. O Truth, Truth, how inwardly did the very marrow of my soul pant for you. . . Yet all the time you were more inward than the most inward place of my heart and loftier than the highest.[12]

In his *Soliloquies* he harks back to this theme in the form of a prayer:

> God, our Father, who exhorts us to pray and who gives us what we ask. Indeed when we pray to you we live a better life and are better. Hear me struggling in these darknesses and give me your right hand. Grant me your light. Call me back. Withdraw me from errors. With you leading, may I return to myself and to you. Amen.[13]

The *redite ad cor*—return to your heart—of Isaiah (46:8) is for Augustine the indispensable condition for contem-plation. In his commentary on the gospel of St John he repeats this saying like a refrain.[14] Prayer is centred in the heart, but in order to see and hear and speak from the heart we have to begin by purifying the soul of sense objects and worldly desires. Otherwise the light of God cannot penetrate and illumine the soul, which is therefore unable to trans-cend itself and advance upwards towards the truth. At present all I have within me is a reflection of the divine wis-dom which constitutes the happy life.

The search for union with God which Augustine describes

so movingly in the first five chapters of Book I of his *Confessions* is primarily the desire to see God in and through the mind, but it is also the yearning to experience the love of God in and with the heart. In Augustine there are three levels of contemplation: the philosophical, the specifically religious, that is the vision of God through the workings of ordinary graces (acquired contemplation), and finally the mystical level which can only be attained through extraordinary graces (infused contemplation). On this level the intellect, will and memory or consciousness remain passive.

But Augustine seldom differentiates. His idea of contemplation is a loving desire for God which is for him the essence of prayer. The heights of contemplation are attainable by all, even by the least, if one perseveres along the road of faith:

> We shall undoubtedly arrive not only at an understanding of incorporeal and immutable things, although in this life not everyone can grasp it, but indeed also at the summit of contemplation, which the apostle says is "face to face" (I Corinthians 13:12). But even the least who walk with the utmost perseverance in the way of faith arrive at this most blessed contemplation.[15]

Whether Augustine can properly be called a mystic, at least in the classical sense of the term, is disputed, but he certainly enjoyed a high degree of contemplation. He says in his *Confessions* that his mind was occasionally raised to a state above its ordinary operations and that he experienced—to quote his own words—"a kind of delight which could it ever be made permanent in me would be hard to distinguish from the life to come".[16] Elsewhere in his *Confessions* he has recorded the famous mystical experience which he shared with his mother, Monica, at Ostia shortly before her death in 387. For one moment as they talked together they transcended their own minds and made direct contact with God:

> While we were thus talking of his Wisdom and pant-
> ing for it, with all the effort of our heart we did for
> one instant attain to touch it; then sighing, and
> leaving the first fruits of our spirit bound to it, we
> returned to the sound of our own tongue.[17]

We may define prayer in Augustinian terms as a search
for God; as a humble, earnest yearning of the soul for union
with him; a fixing of the mind and heart on God in a movement of desire born of love. There takes place in prayer,
wrote Augustine:

> a turning of the heart to him who is always ready to
> give [his light] if we accept what he gives. In this
> turning the interior eye is purified with the exclu-
> sion of the desire of temporal things, so that the
> pupil of the heart (*acies cordis*) may be able to bear
> the pure light of God which shines without ever
> setting or changing. And not only to bear it but also
> to remain in it, not merely with comfort but with
> ineffable joy whereby happiness is truly and really
> perfected.[18]

This short passage contains in a nutshell the celebrated
three stages or states of the spiritual life, the purgative,
illuminative and the unitive. It would carry us far beyond
our immediate object to develop this point. Here the important thing to note is the decisive role which Augustine
assigns to prayer.

Although knowledge or rather the light of faith is fundamental in his teaching on prayer, the emphasis throughout
is on the heart. In describing the affective or unifying
nature of the heart turned to God, Augustine does not
shrink from using the language of human love. Prayer is a
look of loving intent (*affectuosa intentio*). The soul, so to
speak, reaches out to and seeks to embrace and hold God as
would a lover.[19] We speak to God and he speaks to us, but
when we speak it is our heart that speaks: "With the heart
one asks, with the heart one seeks, with the heart one beats,

and it is at the voice of the heart that God opens the door."[20] It is not words that God wants to hear but your heart.

This idea is so central to Augustine's teaching on prayer that he does not hesitate to say that "the whole life of a good Christian is a holy desire."[21] We seek to possess and be possessed by God in an embrace of infinite love. No words can express this longing which wells up from the depth of our being. It is prayer *de profundis*. We never cease to pray, says Augustine, as long as we have this desire for God. Desire establishes immediate, loving contact between the soul and God. It expands the soul which, however, remains insatiable until it sees God face to face and is totally united with him.

Nothing would be more misleading than to conclude that Augustine identifies prayer exclusively with what we may call the prayer of silence. The heart is never silent, just as love can never remain idle. Far from minimising the importance of words in connection with prayer, Augustine attached great importance to formal or set words of prayer. In his writings, for instance *On the gift of perseverance*, he cites prayers from the liturgy, and it is evident that his theology of grace is expressed partly in words taken from the collects of the Mass.[22] Words are important and consequently should not be despised or used lightly. Augustine reminds us that they do help us to express our feelings and formulate our desires, however inadequately.

Not only do words enable us to clarify our thoughts and focus the mind in prayer; they actually stimulate our desire and thereby deepen our prayer: "the more fervent our feeling . . . the more effective our prayer will be".[23] Augustine was not slow to point out that Christ himself prayed in words and prescribed for his disciples a set form of words when they asked him to teach them how to pray. But unless the words come from the heart they are like empty vessels. The directive contained in his rule (2, 3), "What

you say with your mouth turn over in your heart", is
familiar to all.

At the same time he was of the opinion that it is best to
keep one's prayer short. "When you pray," he declared in a
sermon, "what you need is piety, not verbosity."[24] In other
words, one must not confuse, still less identify, prayer with
prayers. Augustine, as we shall see, strongly emphasised the
necessity of our setting aside definite periods for prayer.
One gets the impression from a letter which he wrote in
411-412 that he felt that there would not be much time for
indulging in lengthy prayer if we attend to the necessary
duties of the day.[25] What he had in mind was doubtless
vocal prayers, for he was careful to note that the Lord
spent whole nights in prayer and in his agony prayed all the
longer, though not in many words. The important thing
according to Augustine is that we should concentrate on
trying to preserve an attitude of prayer throughout the day,
even in the midst of worldly occupations.

We fulfil the injunction of St Paul to pray without ceasing
if we sustain the spirit by the continual desire of God which
is preserved and activated by faith, hope and charity. He
cites the example of the Egyptian monks who punctuate
their day by short, repeated dart-like prayers or ejaculations,
thus ensuring that their desire of God did not become
dulled or fade away.[26]

The essential meaning of prayer is often obscured not by
the tendency to indulge in a plethora of words but by our
inability to form words at all. This phenomenon has acquired
the label of "the prayer of stupidity". The expression is unfortunate. Augustine—it is hard to believe that he was ever
at a loss for words—coined the phrase "learned ignorance"
(*docta ignorantia*) which historians of medieval spirituality
usually associate with the Devotio Moderna of the fifteenth
century. There is a difference between stupidity and ignorance. We may be ignorant, says Augustine, but we are not
dumb. Our ignorance is helped by the Spirit who enables us

to pray in a way too deep for words and who instills in us a desire for things beyond our understanding and which consequently we are unable to express in words.[27]

God does not have to listen to our stumbling attempts to formulate words in order that he may know what is in our minds. The fact that we find it difficult to speak to God for any length of time may be a sign from him for silence on our part. What God says to us in prayer is infinitely more important than anything we can say to him. The true servant of God, says Augustine, is a good listener.[28]

He was adamant, however, on regularity as an essential element of prayer-life, that is the setting aside of fixed times for prayer. This is perhaps more difficult to achieve today than ever before. One may adduce as an excuse the specious maxim "to work is to pray" (*laborare est orare*). There is of course a sense in which this statement is valid. Augustine actually says that we speak to God through our works. But to apply the maxim without qualification inevitably leads to a lack of balance in our spiritual life. We need here above all to get our priorities as religious right. We shall do so if we rephrase the adage to read as follows: pray and work (*ora et labora*).[29]

It goes without saying that the spiritual value of our work depends on prayer or rather the grace of God working in and through us, and for this grace we must pray. It is a matter of common experience that if we fail to eat regularly and continue in this way long enough we eventually lose the taste for food. It is exactly the same with prayer. If we do not pray regularly we lose the taste for prayer, and then we abandon the practice of praying. Finally we lose the memory of prayer.

Nothing pained Augustine more as bishop than the inroads which his manifold duties as bishop made on his time for prayer. "We have hardly time to draw our breath," he wrote.[30] The needs of the Church and his people, especially the weakest, and even pagans in distress, compelled him to forego his own preference. For myself, he wrote, "I would much prefer every day at certain hours, as is the rule in well-ordered monasteries, to so some manual work and devote the rest of my time to reading and prayer or the study of sacred Scripture."[31]

He longed for what he euphemistically called "holy leisure" (*otium sanctum*), namely freedom for prayer and study, but he had to sacrifice his love of the truth (*charitas veritatis*) to the necessity of charity (*necessitas charitatis*).[32] Even so, he did make it a point of setting aside fixed times for prayer lest the desire of his heart "having grown luke-warm, might freeze up altogether and become totally extinct unless frequently rekindled".[33] How much time Augustine managed to spend in prayer we do not know. His intimate friend and biographer, Possidius, informs us that he worked during the day and prayed at night. He cannot have had much sleep and it is little wonder that he suffered from insomnia. The mystery is that he managed to accomplish more, in fact, than the printed page, impressive as it is, suggests. Possidius may be excused for doubting whether any one scholar could read and digest all that Augustine wrote.[34]

It is most disappointing, however, that he did not produce one work for which he was eminently fitted, namely a treatise containing the finished expression of his thought on prayer. In this field he was *facile princeps*.[35] The closest he ever got to composing a treatise on prayer is a long letter which he wrote to a widow of high rank, Lady Proba, who asked him to explain for her the meaning of Romans 8:26: "We do not know what we should pray for as we ought." His advice was typical of the man. "Pray," he told her, "for a happy life."[36]

Happiness for Augustine was an abiding question. Indeed one of the first books which he wrote after his conversion was *On the happy life*. Many philosophers, he said in his letter to the good lady, have studied this problem and have given different answers; but Scripture has said all that need be said and in one sentence: "One thing I have asked of the Lord; this I will seek after: that I may dwell in the house of the Lord all the days of my life" (Psalm 26:4).[37] "The one true and only happy life," he added, "is that we, immortal and incorruptible in body and spirit, may contemplate the delight of the Lord for eternity."[38] This should be the end of all our prayers, whatever their specific object may be, for in possessing God we have all that we desire. His peace so surpasses all understanding that we may indeed be said to pray for what we do not know.

Augustine's personal history and his astounding knowledge of the Scriptures convinced him of the absolute necessity and value of intercessory prayer. It would seem to have constituted the whole of his hope. A profound and true sense of humility lay at the root of his genuine feeling of inadequacy. If so, he had the most absolute trust in the goodness and power of God, manifested above all in Christ the mediator, together with an unshakable conviction that if God gives the grace he, Augustine, weak as he confessed himself to be, could do whatever God commanded. The Council of Trent canonised his teaching that God never commands the impossible, but when he does command he orders us to do what we can and to ask for what we are unable to do.[39] In technical language, we must pray for "efficacious graces", the graces necessary for salvation, the greatest being the gift of final perseverance which cannot be merited.

According to St Thomas, following St Augustine, we pray for what are called efficacious graces when we say the Our Father. For Augustine the Lord's Prayer is not only the prayer of petition *par excellence* but the epitome of all prayers. It includes everything that we need to and should pray for. Augustine relates all prayers, including the psalms, to the seven petitions of the Our Father, and warns that it is wrong to add anything to the Lord's own words.[40] Christ, he wrote, gave us the Our Father as a rule of prayer;

hence we must not violate the rule by either adding anything to what it prescribes or omitting any part of it.[41]

If proof be needed of the unique rôle which Augustine assigned to the Our Father it is sufficient to note that he produced at least six expositions of the prayer, the most extensive being in connection with his commentary on the Sermon on the Mount.[42] The earliest explicit reference by Augustine to the Lord's Prayer occurs in the treatise *On the master*, which is a transcript of a conversation between himself and his son, Adeodatus, in 389 at Tagaste (Souk-Ahras). They were discussing the use and significance of words, when Augustine said to the precocious boy—Adeodatus was then about sixteen: "Does it not strike you that the greatest of masters taught his disciples certain words when he instructed them how to pray?" Adeodatus made an important observation in reply: "What he taught them," he answered, "was not words but realities by means of words, so that they should be aware of whom they should pray to and of what they should pray for."[43]

Augustine's reflections on the Our Father constitute a spirituality in themselves.[44] Here I should like to underline one particular aspect—the Our Father as an expression of Christian social love (*amor socialis*).[45] When a Christian says "Our Father" he does not pray just for himself. He does not pray alone. He does not say "My Father". He prays that God will share his gifts with others as well as himself. The Our Father is the prayer of the whole Church, head and members, the *totus Christus*, Augustine's magnificent dictum. In a passage which should by now be familiar—it is incorporated almost in full in the introduction to the new breviary—Augustine declares:

> God could not have given men a greater gift than to make his Word by whom he created all things their head and incorporate them in him as members, so that he is Son of God and son of man; one God with the Father, one man with men. . . He prays for us

as our priest; he prays in us as our head; he is prayed
to by us as our God. Let us recognise therefore our
voices in him and his voice in us. . . We talk with him
and he speaks with us. . . He is prayed to in the form
of God, he prays in the form of a slave: there the
creator, here the created, not changed but assuming
the creature to be transformed. . . and making us
one man with him, head and body. . . Let us therefore pray to him, through him and in him. We speak
with him and he speaks with us. We speak in him, he
speaks in us. . . Do not say anything without him
and he will not say anything without you.[46]

In this way our prayer is always heard by the Father because
it is the prayer of his own well-beloved Son.

It does not follow that God grants our request immediately, even when what we ask for is in conformity with his
will which is always for our good, since he is our good
Father. He may be slow to give, says Augustine, but this
does not mean that he refuses his gifts. When he delays he
does so in order that we may appreciate his gifts and in
order to increase our desire, so that we may be able to
receive what he gives. What he is prepared to give is truly
great, but as yet we are not big enough to hold it![47] Our
hearts will be enlarged the deeper our faith, the firmer our
hope and the more ardent our desire.[48]

We do not know much about Augustine's method of
praying. It may be taken for granted that he did not practise
meditation in the formal sense of the term. Mental prayer is
a comparatively late development in the history of Christian
spirituality. Nonetheless, Augustine's meditations were
indeed profound, as profound as those of the greatest
mystics and in some respects even more profound.

Few artists have perhaps caught as well as Botticelli
Augustine in a moment of meditation. The famous painting,
now preserved in the refectory of the Franciscan convent of
Ognissanti at Florence, depicts Augustine in his scriptorium,
seated at his writing desk. Suddenly a thought strikes him.

He stops, places his right hand over his heart, and gazes with intensity straight ahead. Augustine was human too like all of us. In his *Confessions* he speaks of things which distracted him in his prayers, and records how curiosity one day forced him to stop in the middle of serious thought to watch a dog chasing a hare.[49]

What is certain is that the Scriptures were his meditation book. So thoroughly did he master the sacred page that he literally knew the Bible by heart. Whether dictating (most if not all of his works were dictated) or preaching he was never at a loss for the apt quotation. It has been estimated that some 30,000 explicit quotations occur in his writings, some being of considerable length, from the New Testament alone, not to mention an unlimited number of implicit references. He had of course a prodigious memory and it has actually been suggested that if the Bible had been lost in Augustine's day he could have rewritten the whole from memory without undue effort! What did he find in the scriptures? The short answer is that he found everything. Scripture was for him the mirror of God and the heart of Christ.[50] The liturgy was the second major source of his meditations; but his favourite reading matter were the psalms and the gospel of St John. Even as a catechumen the psalms made a powerful and lasting impression on him.[51] On his death-bed he asked for nothing more than to be left alone to meditate on the seven penitential psalms.

There is one aspect of Augustine's teaching on prayer which is of prime significance for all religious, namely community prayer. In Augustine's view it is the perfect expression of community life whose ideal is *anima una et cor unum in deum*.[52] In order to grasp the essential rôle which Augustine assigned to this form of prayer, we should have to consider it within the context of his wider concept of the monastic life. To attempt to do so here would mean overstepping our terms of reference.

A word may be said, however, about a form of prayer

which has quite a vogue today. I refer to charismatic prayer. One of the cardinal principles of Augustine's teaching on prayer is that it is the Spirit which inspires us to pray and indeed makes prayer possible. If one is to be a man of prayer, one must try to live by and in the Spirit. We do this, says Augustine, if we keep charity, love truth and desire unity.[53] As far as I am aware (I may well of course be mistaken), Augustine never discussed one of the problematic aspects of charismatic prayer, namely speaking in tongues. He points out more than once, however, that when the gift of tongues was originally given with the outpouring of the Holy Spirit, it was given as a sign or in anticipation of something that would be fulfilled later on.[54] He was referring to the spread of the Gospel, the expansion of the Church and its universal unity. The gift of tongues signified that people of all languages would come to believe in Christ, and that the Church would one day speak in the tongues of all mankind. Since this is now an accomplished fact—Augustine needless to say was thinking of the world, the *orbis terrarum*, of his day—the phenomenon no longer occurs. *Signa erant tempori opportuna*: "the signs were suited to the time".[55] But on one point he was adamant. The gift of tongues was certainly a sign of the presence of the Holy Spirit, but it is equally true that the Spirit is present in everyone at baptism. "If you want to know," says Augustine, "whether you have the Spirit, ask your heart. . . If the love of the brother is there, have no doubt."[56] The presence of this Spirit is certified not by tongues but by facts.[57]

Actually Augustine had a very open mind about new or unusual practices. In one of his letters he explains that there is one very helpful rule with regard to such matters. Novelties are not to be condemned but rather encouraged, as long as they are not contrary to faith or morals and are an aid to a holier form of life.[58] We need not be surprised, on the other hand, that he was firmly opposed to the idea of a "pneumatic" church or a church of the spirit. This concept was first introduced by Montanus (c. 174), the father of the montanist heresy. Eusebius had charged him with speaking in tongues contrary to the tradition of the apostolic Church. Montanus had indeed seceded from the catholic Church, or what would be termed today the institutional Church, and formed his own church of the spirit. Augustine would obviously have regarded with suspicion any form of prayer that smacked of montanism. It would be wrong, however, to conclude that he would have frowned on charismatic prayer as practised by well-balanced Christian groups of our time. We may conclude, going on the principle stated above, that he would have approved of it, on condition that it does not lead to divisions or produce elitist groups in the Church, that is so-called "spirituals", but on the contrary leads to an increase of charity. The Spirit is present where there is "love of peace, unity and the Church, spread throughout the world."[59]

M. Benedict Hackett, OSA

2 St Bernard

His life, times and spirituality

The six centuries from the death of St Benedict in 458 to that of St Bernard in 1153 are called, with some inaccuracy but with good reason, the monastic centuries. During that time monasticism became an integral part of society. It affected society at every level, liturgical, spiritual, cultural, economic and whatever. And that surely was an odd situation: that the marginal should become the norm, that the eccentrics should be at the centre! As usually happens, before things got better they got a good deal worse, because for thirty years, from 1123 to 1153, a monk was the most influential person in Western Europe. It may help to give some examples of what his influence was, what it effected.

Cluny had been going for a few centuries. The church at Cluny was the largest of its day and for a long time after, so that when they went to build St Peter's they expressly built it a little larger than the church at Cluny. Yet here was Bernard in his young days as an abbot of a small monastery that belonged to a very small order "taking on" this great colossus of an abbey and order. He did not intend to criticise Cluny, but evidently it got about that he had some notions that Cluny did not approve of. So a certain Benedictine persuaded him to put some of his objections to Cluny on paper. We will not go into these objections; the basic one was that Cluny, even if it had slipped down the road to laxity somewhat, had done something much worse. It had forgotten the meaning of monastic life. It was not a case of

41

mere regulations, mere customs, mere deviations even, but the loss of the purpose of monastic life.[1] And the wonder was that this critic of Cluny was able to convert, not only the Abbot of Cluny, but the whole order of Cluny.

Another instance of his influence, and this time on the western Church of that time, was that he was able to persuade the King of England, Henry I, King Louis of France, and Emperor Lothair of Germany to accept Innocent as the true Pope. Yet another—not very happy in its obvious consequences—was that Bernard, at the orders of Pope Eugene III, a former novice at Clairvaux, launched the second crusade single-handed. Rather astonishing behaviour, one might say, for a man who had retired from the world, even from a world where monasticism was somehow at the centre.

He is regarded as the first of the great autobiographical mystics. In an age of great letter-writers he stands easily supreme, and is still very readable, still quite stimulating and, indeed, an historical source. As a Latinist, he is reckoned the best between Pope St Leo the Great and Petrarch. The monk, the abbot, the reformer and the theologian of his day, he was, in a kind of Elijah fashion, a fire and a portent.[2]

The name of Elijah reminds us that not only was Elijah a great prophet; he had his moments of weakness. You remember how he ran away because a certain queen threatened to put an end to his activities on this earth. Elijah got scared, and yet it was this very running away that brought him to Horeb and that wonderful experience of God. In Bernard's case there was something similar.

Bernard in his young days is described as both shy and studious, and on the other hand as both sociable and affectionate. And this love of study, this curiosity which never deserted him, however he purified it, however he rectified it, nearly proved his undoing monastically speaking. His friends and members of his own family nearly persuaded him not to run away to Citeaux; what kept him from running away, what at least stopped him, what prevented him from devoting himself to mere scholarly pursuits was the thought and memories of his mother. As Jezebel put Elijah on the way to Horeb, so Aleth, the mother of Bernard of Fontaines, put him, if not on the way to Citeaux, at least off the way to mere study. What put him on the way to Citeaux is the subject we are about to discuss.

Bernard was on his way to visit his brothers when he resolved this problem of his, this difficulty in deciding what to do, by turning into a wayside chapel and falling into prayer. It is the first time that any of his early biographers describe Bernard as praying. He went into that church very doubtful about what he would do, very doubtful about whether he could do what he ought to do, but he came out with his mind made up. He would become a monk and a monk of that small, rather hopeless place called Citeaux. But typically, he would not merely take himself to Citeaux. If his friends could not bring him their way, he would bring them his way. And so he retired to Citeaux, to solitude, with plenty of company.

Citeaux, as you may remember, was noted for austerity, for hard fasting, hard manual labour. But the great penance of Citeaux has always been and, please God, always will be, solitude. The brothers were cut off from externs by enclosure, and from one another, to a great extent, by silence. And here was Bernard's opportunity; here also was the great hazard. How could he satisfy his lively mind, his curiosity? How could his thirst for knowledge find satisfaction in such a situation?

He mortified his outward senses, he kept his eyes down, he even plugged his ears so as not to hear too much when he was in the parlour or passing by. But above all he filled his mind, and filled it with the Bible. He read far more than the Bible, but in some sense he never read, never studied, never enjoyed any other reading. He became so well

acquainted with its very phraseology, he knew it so well
that he could hardly write a sentence, he could hardly think
a thought without thinking it in the way the Bible would
say it.

It is amusing for those of us who have spent quite a few
years in a monastery and have got nowhere, to realise that
Bernard only spent three years at Citeaux. Those three
years, though, remind me of a phrase that turned up in a
film of the thirties. Marlene Dietrich asks Gary Cooper how
long he has been in the Foreign Legion and he answers,
"Three years, and they're like three centuries". Bernard's
three years were like three centuries, three centuries of
advance, until he reached a high plateau from which he
never came down. He may have slipped here and there, but
he never really came off the high plateau that he called
"devotio".[3] It is a state, a sabbath of the mind; being untroubled in the midst of troubles, running with joy unspeak-
able in the way of God's commandments.

And after those three years he was sent to found Clairvaux. The valley of Wormwood was to become the valley
of glory, the valley of light. As usual he did not go alone;
he took plenty of his family. Of the twelve that went with
him, four were brothers, one was an uncle and two were
cousins. And he would have had plenty to do merely to
succeed in getting Clairvaux going. But the brethren decided
to send him to a local bishop to get him blessed as abbot
and, as some hold, ordained to the priesthood. And you get
that funny Laurel and Hardy scene. They sent along with
this gaunt and abstracted-looking young man a fine, healthy,
handsome monk, a sort of credit to the diet. The bishop's
household were convinced that it was a case of the well-
kept abbot bringing some unhealthy monk out for a spot of
fresh air. The bishop, as the story goes, discovered otherwise. He discovered that Bernard had plenty of wisdom to
communicate once he was properly tapped. And from then
on Bernard, who would not have much peace in any case, as

an abbot, had even less because, not believing that monks should be exempt from episcopal control, he believed that he ought to obey the bishops of God's Church, and if they wanted him either above the Rhine or below the Alps, he had to be there.

When we think of the glories of his "devotio", of his marvellous fidelity to grace, which, as he was always recommending, he kept up by a tremendous, healthy fear of God, we must not forget that he made mistakes, that he had lapses, that he was not impeccable.

To give some instances of these mistakes. An abbot of a young monastery, a young abbot too, was having great trouble in being an abbot. Bernard recommended to him various things and, above all, he recommended that he stop writing. And here is how he put it:

> [Because] I cannot see you, I mourn for you as lost to me. And so, when on top of all this you, who should be a staff to support me, use your faint-heartedness as a staff with which to belabour me, you are piling sadness upon sadness, one cross upon another. Although it is a mark of your affection for me that you hide none of your troubles from me, it is, nevertheless, unfeeling of you not to spare me, who feel as I do towards you, any details of your sufferings. Why should you make me, who am anxious enough about you, even more anxious? Why should my heart, already torn by the absence of my son, be wounded still more by having to hear every detail of the trials he is enduring? I have shared my burdens with you as with a son and indispensable and faithful helper. But is this the way you help me to carry them? You are not helping to carry them at all, but adding to their weight, and by so doing you are making things more difficult for me without helping yourself.[4]

So the young abbot quietened down.

Between two and nine years afterwards Bernard wrote again:

I had hoped, dearest son, to find a remedy for my worrying over you in not being told of your difficulties. I remember I wrote to you. . . that although it was a mark of your affection towards me that you should hide none of your troubles from me, it was, nevertheless, unfeeling of you not to spare me, feeling towards you as I do, anything of the details.

But now I confess I feel my anxiety for you increased by the very thing I had hoped would relieve it. Hitherto I have only feared or grieved over what you told me, but now there is hardly an evil that could happen which I do not fear for you. In fact, as your favourite Ovid says, "When have I not, by fear, made dangers greater than they were?"

Uncertain about everything, and therefore anxious about everything, I experience real sorrow for imaginary ills. A mind under the influence of love is no longer master of itself.[5]

And here is an instance of what might be regarded as a worse fault. The second abbot of Clairvaux's first daugher-house had a problem: what to do with a monk who kept running away? According to the rule, the abbot should only welcome back such a one three times and after that he should be told where to go. Anyway, Bernard recommends this abbot to be merciful, to humble himself before the unfortunate brother and so help this brother to persevere. And in order to help this abbot to humble himself, this is what Bernard says:

One day I commanded with angry voice and threatening looks my brother Bartholomew (he died since) to leave the monastery, he had so upset me. He immediately betook himself to one of our granges and remained there.

When I found out where he was, I wanted to recall him, but he said that he would not come back unless he was first reinstated in his old position and not put in the last place as if he had been a runaway. He had been turned out of the monastery, he said, without consideration and without his case being heard. As he had not been given a fair trial when he was turned out, he ought not be made submit to punishment prescribed by the rule when he came back.

As I could not trust my own judgment in the matter, owing to my natural feelings about it, I submitted it to the consideration of the brothers. And they, when I was absent, ruled that the brother should not be subjected to the discipline of the rule on being received back, as his expulsion had not been according to the rule.[6]

And that in the Middle Ages before democracy, real or phoney, broke out!

Bernard had quite a good sense of humour. Just one instance. A nun who wanted to be a hermit wrote to Bernard for counsel. She evidently didn't know that Bernard was not frightfully keen on hermits. He was a cenobite and thought that if cenobites behaved themselves they had every chance of becoming as holy as hermits, or maybe more so. So Bernard, after diplomatically stating that of course he could not pronounce on the case very well, not knowing enough facts, suggests in the first place that maybe she was only running away in order not to be under the abbess's orders, but gradually, in a nice way, he settles her case in a few seconds. "You are either a foolish or a wise virgin. If a foolish one, you need your community. If a wise one, your community needs you."

During these years when he was running a monastery that in its heyday held one hundred novices, he had ten very busy years on account of the schism caused by Piereleone and his supporters from 1128 to 1138. And it was during those very years—in 1135—that he began his famous sermons on the *Song of Songs*. Rather odd, that a monk take the *Song of Songs* as background music for his best work. It is good to remember that the *Song of Songs*

was the book most commented upon by monks in the
Middle Ages; Bernard wasn't doing anything unusual in
that. The wonder, however, is that he found time, that he
had an inclination to devote himself to it. He had about a
year, from the Advent of 1135 to January or so of 1137 in
which to get his masterpiece under way. He was not very
well at the time, but at least he had some sort of leisure
when he was left to himself by the more considerate
brethren. What he noted in the *Song of Songs* were three
points: A kind of Fairy Prince, "beautiful above the sons of
men". He is very fond of a dusky yet lovely damsel. She is
very fond of him. Both are crazy about each other, yet the
ups and down of love impinge. At the times she wants him
most, she finds him least; at others, without looking for
him at all, he turns up; and all that kind of thing. It reflected Bernard's thoughts, his own spiritual life, particularly its
most intense moments.[7]

Here is a rather long sample of some of the points he
makes in his sermons on the *Song of Songs*. Naturally he
speaks a lot about love, which is all very fine; as Bernard
would say, "it is great stuff, if it returns to its source",[8]
and if it is in right order.

> "He set love in order in me." A most necessary
> thing. Zeal without knowledge is a thing unsupport-
> able. And the more ardent the zeal the greater is the
> necessity that it be accompanied by discretion, to
> which it belongs to regulate love.
> Zeal without knowledge, instead of being efficacious
> or useful, generally turns out to be extremely perni-
> cious. Consequently, my Brothers, according as our
> zeal grows hotter, our fervour more intense, and our
> love more full, it is necessary that the light of know-
> ledge also should proportionately increase. For it is
> the function of knowledge to moderate zeal, to
> regulate fervour, and to set love in order. . . Indeed,
> it is discretion that sets all the virtues in order, from

which order are derived both their limits and their loveliness, yes, and their stability. . . Discretion, as a result, is not so much a distinct virtue as the governor and guide of every virtue, the regulator of the affections, and the teacher of morals. Take away this and virtue becomes vice. Take away this and the very affections implanted in us for the perfection of our nature, turning aside from their purpose, begin at once to work for the disturbance and ruin of our nature. . .

"He set love in order in me!" Would to God that my own little stock of love were likewise set in order by him who gave it, the Lord Jesus! So should I keep faithful watch over all his interests, but in such a way that what I recognise as belonging most particularly to my duty and office, should have my first attention. Yet although this must engage me before everything else, there are many other matters which, while not concerning me personally in any especial way, ought nevertheless to appeal more strongly to my affections. For that which ought to be the first object of our solicitude need not always of necessity have the strongest claim on our love. Indeed, it is often the case that what should get precedence as regards our care and attention, is less conducive to our advancement, and must, therefore, be less attractive to our love. In other words, our reason must often give second place in esteem to what duty requires us to put first in solicitude. But that which obtains the preference from right reason, rightly ordered love would have us embrace more affectionately.

For example, am I not obliged, in virtue of my position, to have care of you all? Now, were I to devote myself to any other object with so much attention that I could no longer exercise properly the office of superior, I should most certainly offend against the claims of good order; even though I appeared to be actuated by a motive of love (charity).

On the contrary, if I am faithful in giving my first
attention, as I am bound to do, to the duties of my
office, yet do not experience a greater joy at the
greater progress in divine love which I observe
another to be making, it is plain that my love is in
one part rightly ordered, wrongly in another.

But if I make that for which I am most specially responsible the object of my most special solicitude,
and at the same time feel myself more strongly
attracted to what is of greater worth, then, without
doubt, my love shall be found perfectly regulated
and there shall be nothing to prevent me from
saying, "He set love in order in me."[9]

And now he passes from the contrast, and the necessary
complementarity, between knowledge and love, to the complementarity between affective and effective love.

Is love to be affective or effective? Both, surely, but
in opposite ways. For the latter loves best what is
low, the former prefers what is high. It cannot be
questioned, for example, that in well-ordered affective love the love of God takes precedence of the
love of one's neighbour, and, among men, the more
perfect are preferred to the less perfect, heaven is
preferred to earth, eternity to time, the soul to the
body. But well-regulated active love moves in the
inverse order, if not always, as a rule. . .Who can
deny that in prayer we converse with God? Yet how
often are we not obliged to interrupt and abandon
it. . . for the sake of those who need the help of our
words or works! . . . How often, without prejudice
to conscience, do we not put aside our reading in
order to devote ourselves to manual labour? How
often are not our temporal concerns more than
sufficient reason for putting off the celebration of
the very Mass itself! Surely a preposterous order.
But necessity recognises no law. . .

The case is very different with affective love. . . For
it is wisdom by which we value things in accordance

with their worth. . .

Give me a man who above all and with his whole being loves God, and proportions his love of himself and of his neighbour to his own and his neighbour's love for God; who loves his enemies in the hope that they will at length recover the grace of divine love; who loves his parents with tenderness, by the instinct of nature, and his spiritual guides with the gratitude that comes of grace; and whose well-ordered love for God extends itself in like manner to all the other creatures of God; who. . . "uses this world as if he used it not", and by interior spiritual taste can so distinguish between what is meant to be employed as a means and what must be embraced as an end, that he uses things transitory in a passing way and only for as long as they are useful; while he longs for the things of eternity with an insatiable desire—give me, I say a man like this, and I will confidently declare him wise with the wisdom which esteems all things at their proper worth; he may boast with all justice, he has the right to say and say unhesitatingly, "He has set love in order in me."[10]

What about action and contemplation?

It is the characteristic of true and pure contemplation that it not only inflames the soul with the fire of divine love, but it also occasionally fills it with such zeal and desire to gain others to God who shall love him as it loves him itself, that it gladly interrupts its contemplative repose and devotes itself to the labour of preaching. Afterwards, having satisfied this longing, at least to some extent, it returns to solitude with all the more eagerness in proportion as it knows that its interrupting it has been fruitful.[11]

You will notice the return to contemplation, with all the more, not with less desire.

In the summer of 1153, Bernard was feeling ill. He could neither eat nor sleep, his legs were quite swollen and he knew, as those who are about to die know, that the end was near. Yet he wrote to one of his friends and he had you might say, his last little joke, one of his deliberate distortions of Scripture. Referring to what our Lord said, "The spirit is willing but the flesh is weak", he wrote, "The spirit is willing in spite of the weak body."

And now we may ask, has Bernard any perceptible influence today? Is he of any use? In fact, he is more popular in certain circles today that he ever was because of what Dom Jean Leclerc has defined as "monastic theology". And to explain monastic theology, a little story may be in order. It happens to be a true story.

An American Benedictine abbot met a European Benedictine and was telling him with some amazement that one of his monks, an American of the 20th century, had fallen in love with the writings of St Gregory the Great. This American abbot really could not get over it. The European monk could understand very well what had happened, but he said nothing. He agreed that it was rather strange. Years passed and the European monk met the American abbot and what was his amusement and amazement to discover that the American abbot had himself fallen in love with the writings of St Gregory the Great! Saint Gregory was a monk for some of his life (he does not seem to have been a Benedictine), and monks have always found him extremely useful. Why? He has a spirit, he has an atmosphere, he has ideals which monks have always found to be congenial. And that helps to explain perhaps why monastic theology has a certain actuality, a certain permanence among monks. Because monastic theology, like all theology, comes from a situation and applies to a situation. Revolutionary South American theology arises out of the situation down there and they try to apply it down there. Monastic theology arises in monasteries—monks use it and apply it to their monastic life. All theology is truly one. All Christian theology agrees, basically. All branches of it can help one another, while differing. Patristic theology differs, to some extent, from monastic theology and monastic theology differs from scholastic theology. Patristic and monastic theology are closer to each other than are monastic and scholastic. Comparing monastic and scholastic theology we get points like this: monastic theology is patristic rather than philosophical; it looks back to the Fathers rather than reasoning about faith. Monastic theology is personal, scholastic strives for accuracy and abstraction. . Monastic theology is prayer-fostering rather than practical or even pastoral. Monastic theology prefers life to light.

Here is another instance of how Bernard can be pertinent in monastic situations. A Carthusian died in 1957, and you could not imagine (remembering the Carthusians, with their great tendency to live the hermit life—nineteen hours a day by themselves in a cell) a monk of that breed interested in the most cenobitic of monks. And yet this Carthusian seems to have preferred Bernard to all the spiritual writers of his Order. And not only that; he is able to quote and refer to a 17th century Carthusian who on his deathbed, when he had a bit of strength left and wanted to do a bit of reading, asked for his book and when his assitant, the infirmarian or whoever he was, handed him the Bible he said, "No, give me Bernard." And it happened to be Bernard on the *Song of Songs*!

Here is an extract from the first sermon on the *Song of Songs*; it gives some idea of the essence of the existential monastic theology in St Bernard:

> The *Song of Songs* is called the Song of Songs because it is the fruit of all the rest [all those other songs of thanksgiving that Bernard had already referred to in this sermon] . Grace (*unctio,* anointing) alone can teach it, nor can it be learned save by experience. It is for the experienced, then, to recognise it, and for others to burn with desire, not so much of knowing as of experiencing it; this song is not noise of the mouth but jubilee of heart; not

sound of lips but a tumult of interior joys; not a
symphony of voices, but a harmony of wills. It is
not heard outside, for it sounds not externally. The
singer alone can hear it and he to whom it is sung. . .
[the soul and the divine Word] celebrating the
chaste and joyous embraces of loving minds, the
concord of wills and the union resulting from reci-
procal affection.

Bernard's greatest achievement, undoubtedly, was that
he became a monk, became a very good one, and remained
one, in spite of all the incentives he got to become a bishop,
or a missionary, or a preacher. He remained a monk. Cenobites are monks who live in community and one of their
great tendencies is to become terribly practical, to become
frightfully useful and in that way to run away from solitude,
for solitude is a waste of time for those who don't want to
be monks. But St Bernard once and for all recalled cenobites
to the fact that the personal search for God in solitude
defines, sanctifies and brings a monk to the purpose of his
existence.

Bernard and prayer

Downside Abbey means different persons to different people. On monastic history and spirituality there are Abbot Cuthbert Butler and Dom Hubert van Zeller; on early liturgy there is Dom Hugh Connolly; chant, Gregorian and Grail have an expert in Dom Gregory Murray; Vatican II finds a good exegete in, as he used to be, Abbot B. C. Butler; Dom Illtyd Trethowan provides what may be described as a monastic existential philosophy. No doubt each of these sons of Saint Benedict would be able to tell you something about prayer. For present purpose, however, the pertinent Downside names are Abbots Lambert Ramsey and John Chapman. Dom John succeeded Dom Lambert as Abbot and, such is the way with popes and abbots, differed notably from his immediate predecessor, not only during prayer but when it came to discussing it. Abbot Chapman was forever talking and writing about prayer; Abbot Ramsey did not even mention prayer in his weekly addresses to his community. Benedictines as a rule leave theories about Saint Benedict's Rule to others. Abbot Lambert seems not only to have taken Saint Benedict's advice about being deeply recollected during the divine office, he also followed his directive about going into the oratory and simply praying.

But what has all this to do with Saint Bernard and prayer? It is a reminder that while the mouth tends to speak of what fills the heart, the heart can keep its secrets from mouth and manuscript. And all the more so if what fills the heart is seen, not so much as prayer and desire, but as love. Saint Bernard's great passion was the love of God. This explains his devoting so little of his writing to our Lady; only some three per cent, it has been calculated. How much he gives to prayer as such, what he usually calls "oratio", has not been measured; it could be as little as half of three per cent.

No wonder Cistercians like Lehodey and Belorgey have, with all respect, not much use for our man of Clairvaux! Abbot Lehodey in his *The Ways of Mental Prayer* mentions Saint Bernard very seldom, and only when dealing with the mystical stages of prayer. Abbot Belorgey in *The Practice of Mental Prayer* has a section entitled, "The Mysticism of Saint Bernard"; otherwise there is no mention of the saint.

Obviously not much help is to be had from these authors. Perhaps, instead of reading *about* the writings of the saint, if we have a look at his writings something may emerge to enlighten and encourage us.

Saint Bernard and his contemporaries lived in a much tidier, tinier world than ours, yet spiritually they seem to have lived in a much larger universe. They did not have to wait for Teilhard de Chardin to tell them of the big picture of God's plan. Saint Paul had made them aware of the way things were really going. The Abbot of Clairvaux often uses and discusses that text from the Letter to the Romans: "Those whom he predestined he also called; and those whom he called he also justified; and those whom he justified he also glorified." Our position at present is in the "called" and "justified", in the link between predestination and glorification. Predestined from eternity, we are called and justified in time in order to be glorified in eternity. Prayer comes right here in the "called" and "justified". For "the Spirit himself assures our spirit that we are the children of God",[1] and enables us "to cry out 'Abba, Father!'" precisely because the Spirit is predestination: "The Spirit proceeding from the Father and the Son predestines us"[2] or, if anything more emphatically, "The Holy

Spirit is the love in which we are predestined."[3]

This makes predestination personal and vital in the highest sense, and makes sense of the idea that willingness to listen to the word of God is the surest sign of predestination: "He who is of God listens to the words of God." Which is a reminder to listen today if we should hear God's voice, and also that predestination is outside our control; it is objective; it is there whether we listen or not, pray or not.

Another personal and vital process outside our control, implied in and flowing from predestination, is God's going ahead, the anticipation of the Almighty. God is always first, always ahead of us: "he loved us first". "God chose us before the beginning of the world", not before we chose him! He anticipates our prayers. "My prayer shall come before you in the morning," says the psalm. Saint Bernard goes on to remark that there would be no prayer at all unless the Spirit first inspired it.[4]

Precisely because they are the words of the Spirit, we should attend to the words of the psalms during the psalmody. That and nothing else is what the Holy Spirit expects from us just then. There must be no exception; even thoughts suggested before an office by one of Saint Bernard's own sermons—he does not hesitate to call the place in which he preaches "a lecture hall of the Holy Spirit"[5] —are, as the late Mr Goldwyn would have phrased it, included out.

The Holy Spirit is ever active in the work of our salvation, but not in a uniform fashion: "The Spirit breathes where he wills" and it is not easy "to know the way he comes or goes". But come he must if we are to pray. "Daily experience proves to us that our prayers come from the Spirit." And God must not merely come, he has to provoke us. By his promises, and with such words as "Ask and you shall receive," God "extorts" from us the prayers that gain us his free gifts.[6] More usually, perhaps especially in the early stages of our journey through the desert, God tricks us into praying by the troubles he sends our way. His whole purpose is that we be "forced" to call to him, that he may have the opportunity to prove to us how true he is to that word of his: "Call to me in the day of trouble; I will deliver you."

Another device that gets us to pray may be called mediation. On the face of it mediation seems ridiculous. No being is more present to us than God, he is our very soul. Why go outside him for help? The fact is that creatures affect us more than God does. "Man has become like the beasts,"[7] he feeds his senses on what is outside, the objects of his affection lie scattered through the world.[8] God has accepted this situation. He has become visible and percept-ible and even pitiable.[9] And he has associated others with him in his saving work. The New Eve has a real part to play, subordinate but similar to the role of the New Adam. At a certain stage it may be psychologically helpful to consider her as all-pitying and a stranger to the severity of the Son to whom all judgment has been given. In reality, however, she, the most predestined in Christ, has been formed in the image of her Son. Just as "there is nothing for man to be scared of in the Son of God, all in him is kind and fatherly",[10] so, "why should frail man tremble in Mary's presence? There is nothing terrible about her; she is all gentleness."[11]

Even our tendency to prefer closeness to us to closeness to God in our friends has been catered for; the saints who have learnt compassion from what they suffered are anxious, in some sense, for our welfare. Were they to forget us, we could still benefit from them even during their life here in this world. A consoling truth, this last, that had the immature, impatient-to-love-God-for-God's-sake Bernard disconsolate. There he was, more affected by the sight or word or even mere memory of some holy person, than by the God whom his soul would love! It taught him not only that such people were on the way to God, but that humility and brotherly love were the way to the love of God whom his soul would love.

Predestination, anticipation, provocation, mediation: the four wheels, so to say, of the bandwagon to beatitude: there they are, outside of us and our control. We cannot beat this movement but, with God's help, we can join it; we can get into it and get it into us; we can climb onto this wagon and stand on and in it with the two "legs" of meditation and prayer. However, before saying something of these two "legs", there is a certain presupposition, something else we have to stand on: faith. It not only enables us to accept the four "wheels"; it ensures that, essentially at least, our meditation and prayer are what they ought to be; and, no less important, it prevents our measuring our meditation and prayer with the wrong yardstick.

Saint Bernard gives, admittedly in terms we are not too familiar with, a vivid illustration of the importance of faith in our prayerful consideration of our incarnate Lord. It is the scene where Isaac blesses Jacob disguised as Esau. Saint Bernard notes that what fooled the blind old man was not the voice, which he recognised as Jacob's, but the feel of Jacob which, because of the bits of goat-skin, he took to be Esau. The holy abbot, never guessing how dull we of the twentieth century would become, does not think it necessary to tell us explicitly that Jacob is taken as a figure of our Lord, disguised in our skins and the likeness of our sins. And Bernard concludes: Isaac, holy patriarch and all though he was, was fooled by his feeling and his fancy and not by his hearing.

Do not be fooled by your feelings and fancies, no matter how highly you may be tempted to rate your experiences. This warning is impressive, coming from one who was delighted that God in Christ had come down to the level of our imagination, from one who held that love of man for God depended, even in Old Testament times, on faith in the Incarnation, and from one who considered a real affection for Christ a great gift of the Spirit. He would have us realise how necessary is the "faith" that "comes from hearing", the wisdom of keeping to "the measure of faith". These last words, "measure of faith" (*rationem fidei*) contain the hint that reason and common sense are by no means to be neglected.

Given this basic foundation and condition, meditation can be as colourful as you like. Saint Bernard has not the slightest inclination to fix on a particular method, no matter what influence his first sermon for advent may have had, with its looking at who comes, from where, to where, for what, when and what way?[12]

And so to the other "leg". But before discussing what the abbot of Clairvaux recommends about praying, a word about the word he prefers for prayer, "oratio". The roots of the word he takes to be "os" and "ratio", "mouth" and "reason".

He writes that prayer (*oratio*) is, as it were, an expression or confession of the mouth. In case we should miss his meaning, he likens prayer to (what he takes to be) the Magdalen's kissing our Lord's feet, confessing with her mouth her faith and need of him.[13]

This scene suggests not only the need for faith and, be it said, for the body—more of this later—but that, under God, prayer depends on the pray-er. Your prayer is what you are. Moses and Philip, and, yes, Thomas made big requests because they were, thanks to the Spirit's influence, big, magnanimous persons. Nor need lesser persons despair of great results for their prayers. The psalm tells us, "Take delight in the Lord and he will give you the desires of your heart." This delight is delight in virtue or, at least, steady exercise of virtue; not some vision of God, but strong virtue for God's sake. And, not least, exercise of faith in prayer. We should value our praying because and as God values it.

Such the "delight", but what are the required "desires"?

They are those "the judgment of reason approves." Here again reason and faith go together. We may ask for what is good for body and soul on condition that what we ask for is needful and really helpful to us in these respects. However, as we easily go astray in these requests, we should be thankful when God refuses to grant our prayers, it means that he truly cares for us.[14] When it comes to asking for beatitude and all that will bring us there, there must be no hesitation.

There must, moreover, be the greatest possible desire for what is desired. Prayer does not escape from the pray-er at this stage, it is "forced" out by sheer need. Saint Bernard, when discussing the necessity of self-knowledge and knowledge of God for the spiritual life, illustrates how conditioned real prayer is by a person's real wants:

> I desire that my soul should learn in the first place to know itself, for this is required by reason both of utility and right order. By reason of good order, since the first object and truth for each is what he is himself. And by reason of utility, because such knowledge does not inflate with pride, but rather humbles us, and is thus an excellent preparation for the spiritual edifice we intend to raise. This edifice cannot remain standing unless it be firmly grounded on the foundation of humility. Now, the soul can find nowhere a more fit and efficacious means for humbling itself than the true knowledge of itself. . . Contemplating itself in the light of truth, it shall discover how far removed it is from the ideal of perfection. Then, groaning in its wretchedness, for its real wretchedness can no longer remain concealed from it, will it not cry out to the Lord, with the Prophet, "In your truth you have humbled me"? How can it help being humbled in this true knowledge of itself, when it sees itself laden with sins, oppressed with the weight of the corruptible body, entangled in worldly cares, polluted with the filth of

carnal desires, blind, earthward stooping, feebled, involved in many errors, exposed to a thousand dangers, agitated by a thousand fears, disquieted by a thousand suspicions, discouraged by a thousand difficulties, burdened with a thousand necessities, prone to vice, indisposed for virtue? . . . Yes, it will be converted to the Lord. It will cry out in its humility, with the Prophet, "Heal my soul for I have sinned against you." And being converted it will receive consolation from the Lord, because he is "the Father of mercies and the God of all consolation."

As for me, my brothers, so long as I look upon myself, "my eye abides in bitterness". But if I lift up my face and turn my gaze to the help of the divine compassion, the depressing sight of my own unworthiness is relieved by the joyous sight of God, and I say to him, "My soul is troubled within myself, therefore will I remember you." Nor is that some mean sight of God which gives us the experience of him as loving and gracious; because in very truth "he is gracious and merciful, patient and rich in mercy . . ." Goodness is his very nature and it is characteristic of him "to show mercy always and to spare". By this experience, therefore, and in this order, God gives us a saving knowledge of himself. Man recognises the helplessness of his condition. He cries to the Lord. The Lord listens and makes answer to him, "I will deliver you and you shall honour me." And thus the knowledge of oneself leads to the knowledge of God. He is perceived by means of his own image, which is renewed in us, while we, confidently "beholding the glory of the Lord with open face, are transformed into the same image from glory to glory, as by the Spirit of the Lord."[15]

To judge from a passage like this, the God Saint Bernard prayed to might seem a slightly sentimental old gentleman. Nothing could be less true. The favourite image our abbot uses, when he uses one, is that from the well-known sixth chapter of *Isaiah*. Here is a good example:

> If recollected in spirit and with a mind sober and free from distracting thoughts, you enter alone into the house of prayer, and standing before God at one of the altars, touch the very gate of heaven with the hand of holy desire, and lifted up by the ardour of your devotion to the choirs of the holy ones, bemoan in their presence the afflictions and sorrows that bother you and . . . confess your needs and implore compassion—if, I say, you act like this, I have too much confidence in the word of him who said, "Ask, and you shall receive," to believe you shall go out empty-handed, provided only that you persevere in knocking.

In this passage reference is made to the old monastic custom of praying at an altar, and to faith and perserverance in prayer. However, there does not appear to be anything that points to *Isaiah*, chapter six. Unless we recall another passage where our saint, commenting on Saint Benedict's advice about reverence at prayer, would have us pray to God "in the presence of the angels and of the assembly of the saints"; and, further on, he tells us that prayer is being taken and presented to him who sits upon a throne "raised high" in the angels, who did not fall at all, and "lifted up" in men picked up, needy and poor, from the dust and the dung-heap.[16] Quite a cenobitic and liturgical kind of God, even for private prayer!

Prayer for Saint Bernard has four stages, that fit conveniently enough under the four headings, supplications, prayers (*orationes*), intercessions and thanksgivings.[17] At first we are so ashamed of ourselves that we are only too glad to ask the prayers of others, as in the litany of the saints. Then, as our conversion becomes steady, we dare to address God "mouth to mouth". After this we dare to pray for others. The highest stage is prayer so high that it

demands mystical graces in the strict sense. Before we take
a look at the meaning of ecstasy for the holy abbot, notice
that these four stages are, as it happens, predestination,
anticipation, provocation and mediation in inverse order,
in a true sense.

You will recall that the Magdalen of *Luke*, chapter seven,
was described as praying with her mouth. This was no mere
quasi-etymology: we need our bodies, our outside, to pray;
in fact, Saint Bernard was of the opinion that we could not
enjoy the beatific vision without our bodies,[18] an idea not
viewed so unfavourably now as, say, twenty years ago. God,
however, and he alone, can affect our minds and wills
directly from within. This is what happens in strictly
mystical prayer. It is not necessarily a case of mind and
will, but can be mind or will; the ideal is, of course, both.

And no wonder. Full union with God means that the
Holy Spirit, the kiss that joins the Father and the Son, im-
presses himself, through the gifts of wisdom and understanding, on the will and mind, the two lips, as it were, of
the soul. Prayer may be a drinking of the Spirit, and even a
getting drunk and forgetting one's fleshy desires, but this is
so far further in the same direction as to seem altogether
different; it is a sleep where God is seen, although only as a
confused reflection in a mirror, in a sudden flash; it is a
very death to the ordinary way of knowing through images;
that mysterious half-hour or so of silence in heaven; a
passing into God—Saint Bernard's description of Saint
Malachy's death, incidentally—deification, in the sense of
becoming and being aware of becoming one spirit with the
Lord; it is an experience, although in faith, of the absolute
future.

It may be doubted whether such a happening would be
called "prayer" by Saint Bernard, but he certainly connects
it with prayer.[19] It may, provided one's spiritual life is
earnest, be prayed for. It leads to prayer, not least when the
love-struck soul, driven half-crazy by the to-and-froing of the

Word, his sudden withdrawings when most sought and surprising appearances when least expected, has no thought or cry but, "Come back, my beloved!"

A person in this category that has really become intimate with the living God, that, in some way, has taken over the business of salvation, is capable of the fourth degree of prayer, is able, like our Lord at the tomb of Lazarus, to thank God for what he is about to give. Such a person experiences the truth of the words, "when you ask for anything in prayer, you have only to believe that it is yours, and it will be granted you."

It is amusing that at one time Saint Bernard seems to have inclined to the notion that many could reach such a high peak in prayer—the Charles Atlases of the spiritual life have a tendency to give us the you-can-have-a-body-like-mine bit. Experience taught him that very few did in fact reach it. It also taught him that they would never fully master even the first degree of prayer. The one sure thing about the perfect, in this world, is that the higher they go, the more convinced they are that they have not reached perfection.[20]

Not being so perfect and so aware of our imperfection as all that, we may find it useful to remember those words of divine promise in the forty-ninth psalm: "Call to me in the day of trouble; I will deliver you." True, in going for what amounts to the second degree of prayer, in Saint Bernard's scheme, we have passed over the holy abbot's so convinced and convincing exhortations to use the holy names of Jesus and Mary in our difficulties, but it will do us no harm to see how he values recourse to prayer amid the ups and downs of a fervent spiritual life, in the case of a soul so intimate with the person of the Word as to dare utter the words, "draw me after you".

> "Draw me after you." Do you not see that he who walks in the Spirit cannot possibly remain always in the same state, nor always advance with the same

facility, and that the way of man is not in his own power, but according as the Spirit is pleased to arrange matters, the soul at one time more sluggishly, at another with greater alacrity, forgetting what it has left behind, presses on to what lies ahead? I think that what now you hear me speaking of exteriorly, you may learn interiorly from your own experience.

Therefore, when you perceive yourself affected with languor, sloth or disgust, do not on that account lose confidence or desist from application to spiritual things. Rather seek for the helping hand, beg to be drawn, until aroused by grace and rendered more alert and active, you will run again and be able to say, "I have run in the way of your commandments once you enlarged my heart."

Yet, when grace is present, enjoy it in such a way as not to fancy you possess it by some inalienable right; do not be so sure of it as if it could never be taken from you. . .

Be not, consequently, too secure in the day of your strength, but with the prophet cry out to God, "When my strength shall fail me, do not forsake me." And similarly take comfort in the time of temptation, saying, "Draw me after you." Thus you shall not lose hope in the evil day, nor foresight in the good. Amidst the prosperity and adversity of this changeful existence you will display, so to speak, an image of changeless eternity, by this unalterable equanimity and unshakable constancy of mind, "blessing the Lord at all times", and . . . gradually bringing yourself to a condition that, to some extent, is one of fixed and stable immutability; while, at the same time, you are beginning to renew and restore in yourself that primordial and glorious likeness to the eternal God, "in whom is no change, no shadow of alteration. . ." By this, I say, the noble, reason-endowed creature, made to the image and likeness of its creator, shows that it is retrieving and recovering the dignity of its earliest honour, in that it deems it unworthy of itself to be conformed to the fashion of this fleeting world, and, rather, strives, according to the injunction of Saint Paul, to be reformed in the newness of its mind, unto the image in which . . . it was created. And thus, as is proper, it will force the world, which was, after all, made for its sake, to conform to itself. For having put off the form of corruption and reassumed the form that is proper and natural to it, "all things shall begin to work together unto good" for it, for they shall recognise the master for whose service and enjoyment they were created.

Hence, I believe that what the only-begotten said of himself, namely, that if he were "lifted up from the earth", he would "draw all things" to himself, can be applied to all his brothers, to those whom the Father "foreknew and predestined to be made conformable to the image of his Son, that he might be the first-begotten among many brothers". Therefore, even I shall make bold to say, that "I, if I be lifted up from the earth, will draw all things to myself". Do not suppose that I act rashly in appropriating to myself the words of one whose likeness I have put on. . . In fact the whole world is the wealth of the faithful soul. The whole of it, yes, because both its adversity and prosperity are equally its servants and cooperate unto good for such a soul.[21]

Here again Saint Bernard stresses faith, despite one's weakness, in predestination, in the Holy Spirit. Notice, however, that prayer is seen as having recourse to God's helping hand. It is not seen as a substitute for personal choice and effort, but as a necessary back-up service that has to be used wisely; one greater than Saint Bernard has told us, "Not every one who calls me Lord, Lord, will enter the kingdom of Heaven." If those who worship health cannot be healthy, those who worship prayer cannot be holy: "Keep your worship for God."

Prayer should, above all, be worship. True, the worship

of God "raised high and lifted up" does tend to remind one of one's insignificance. But it is precisely the realisation and acceptance of one's insignificance that enables one to be lifted up to appreciation of the God who cares so greatly for one so insignificant. Such appreciation is true liberation. It is easy to cast one's cares on the God who so carefully cares for his whole creation, and makes everything cooperate for the good of those who accept his helping hand.

Hugh McCaffery, OSCO

3 St Thomas Aquinas

His life, times and spirituality

One might wonder why St Thomas should feature at all in a gallery of spiritual masters. For several centuries now we have been accustomed to make quite a rigid distinction between theology and spirituality, so that we have not normally expected the practitioners of one to have all that much to say to us about the other. And there is no doubt at all that St Thomas was a theologian. And worse still, I suppose, to modern readers, he was a rather dry, perhaps even a dull theologian, certainly not one of the most readable. We may admire his own piety, his own spirit of prayer, but are we really to turn to him as a master for our own piety?

I would suggest that it is precisely as a theologian that Thomas has something to say to us which can help in our piety and prayer. St Albert, who was St Thomas' teacher, defines theology as *scientia secundum pietatem*, which one can loosely translate as that kind of knowledge that goes with love. And I think that in the view of St Thomas, though he does not define theology in quite those terms, theology is a supremely important element in that friendship with God which we are called to enjoy.

So we shall not just be considering what St Thomas has to say about the spiritual life as such. We shall consider the role theology itself is to play in our lives. And of course the life of St Thomas will be the aptest illustration of his own teaching.

There is one point that must be clarified a bit. This concerns one of the more controversial topics that has arisen in recent years in the Church: the question of religious experience. Our interest in religious experience is no doubt a reflection of an interest that characterises most of our society, an interest in any kind of experience. Experience has become a sort of unchallengable argument, so that when we say, well, I felt it, no one is allowed to ask any more rude questions. And on the other hand experience has become an unqualified Good Thing, so that even when everything goes wrong, we can still console ourselves with the thought that it's all experience, as if somehow that compensated. And students are sometimes encouraged to go out and "get experience"; it really is rather dangerous if one stops to think what that might mean in practice.

Obviously experience is an integral part of living. We are meant to live our lives so that we do experience things. But I wonder whether there isn't a danger that we can fall for a kind of romanticism which focuses on experience without really seeing that experience is always dependent on that of which it is an experience.

A very interesting analysis of what I think is an analogous problem is made in a book called *Passion and Society*, by Denis de Rougement. He analyses particularly the story of Tristan and Isolde, and he suggests, very convincingly, that there is a kind of love that is entirely absorbed in itself. The only thing that is really valued is the experience of loving. You need somebody to spark off the experience. But they must not come too close, because if your love were to reach any kind of real fulfilment, then you would actually lose the experience of it. And it is fascinating to notice, in the case of Tristan and Isolde, that whenever they come within reach of each other, they have to separate themselves from one another. So their love lives off separation, off unfulfilment.

I think a corresponding thing can happen with an interesting experience. It can be a concern simply to feel things in a kind of vacuum, so that it isn't simply an experience of anything except itself; it's an experience of experience.

In mystical theology this question arises very specifically in the form: are we interested in God, or are we interested in our experience of God? Are we interested in God, we may say, even more challengingly, or are we interested in prayer?

In the case of St Thomas, at any rate, there can be no doubt at all. If we look to Thomas to tell us about interesting experiences that he has had, then we look in vain. Which is why the late Dom David Knowles seems to have disqualified him as a mystical writer, a very odd thing to do. But St Thomas was fairly interested in God, if we can believe the story told in his biography. Even at the age of five the young Thomas was bothering his schoolmaster with the question, what is God? And this interest clearly prevailed right through his life. The one thing that really fascinated him was God. When, later on, as we are told, our Lord appeared to him with the words, "You have written well of me, Thomas, what reward do you want?" Thomas answered, "Nothing but you yourself, Lord." He was drawn to God throughout his whole life, so his whole life and his whole teaching are profoundly theocentric. *Deus est finis rerum*, he wrote, "God is what it is all about."

This is not simply an interest in words and ideas about God. St Thomas assures us that a merely rational knowledge of God, such as one might reach through philosophy, could never make us happy. Even the knowledge derived from faith can't quite do that. But it is at least a beginning, because it is a sharing, however dim and inadequate, in God's own knowledge of himself.

Insofar as faith is already a sharing in God's own knowledge of himself, clearly St Thomas must be right in declaring that it reaches through to God himself. He knows very well that faith is concerned with the things we say about

God, the propositions, the formulae that we cannot help but use. But faith doesn't stop there; it reaches through to the living reality of God himself.

But faith suffers from the terrible disadvantage of not being able actually to take possession of its object. Faith can never put God in its pocket. God eludes our grasp in this life. Faith has, as it were, to take him on trust. This is why, in this life, knowing God seems such a poor second to loving God.

Of course many schools of spirituality have declared that loving God is more important than knowing God. But St Thomas won't accept that. For him there is a serious difficulty about making love primary. And his analysis is extremely interesting. He points out that, unless what we are in love with is simply our own love, love is dependent on something else to achieve the fruition of its object. To love someone is not of itself to possess them. And so to love God is not of itself to possess God. To quote St Thomas' own words, "The achievement of one's own end does not consist in the act of the will in itself. The will moves towards the end as to something missing when it desires it, and when its end is present it rests in it with joy, but the desire itself is evidently not the attainment of the end; it is a movement towards the end." Enjoyment of the end comes about when the desired end is present, but not the other way about. Nothing comes to be present simply because the will delights in it. The mere fact that we want something does not automatically guarantee that it is going to be there.

So there must be something other than the act of will which makes present to the will its desired end. In the case of our love for God, what is this something else? In the view of St Thomas it is our intellect. We should be clear that *intellectus*, in mediaeval Latin, does not primarily refer to rational argumentation and that kind of thing. It refers much more directly to our capacity of intuition.

Unlike our restless minds, scurrying about hither and thither, intellect in the scholastic use of the word is essentially a faculty at rest.

There's a text in St John's gospel which is surely very pertinent here and which must have made a profound impression on St Thomas. "In this is eternal life, that they should know thee." The essence of our eternal bliss, it seems, and this is certainly Thomas' view, is that our intellect, our minds, will be utterly filled with the direct knowledge of God.

He says that the final purpose of our creation is intellectual good, and it is in this text that our will finds its own utter contentment. It is this intellectual fruition of God that actually unites us with God.

At first sight this is rather a chilling picture, not a very heart-warming way of talking about our union with God. But if we explore it, taking St Thomas as our master, we will find it quite humane.

We will explore first some of the consequences of this Thomastic primacy of the intellect.

In the first place, we must be clear that Thomas is not simply enthroning human reason without further ado. He is sometimes accused of being a rationalist and this is very unfair. He is as explicit as can be that God utterly transcends our natural grasp. He is our purpose and our end. But he is to us a supernatural purpose. So the mind reaching out towards God is dependent on God reaching out towards the mind.

This is why theology is so terribly important. We are created for union with God, but we cannot realise this goal simply under our own steam. Our mind can only hold God insofar as God gives himself to us. And so our whole spiritual life must be based on faith, on God's revelation of himself.

But this, for St Thomas, does not mean that the natural operations of the mind are simply invalidated. The mind is made for God. The fact that this involves it in a kind of self-transcendence in no way means that its ordinary pursuits and activities are thereby rendered useless. The mind is fulfilled and enhanced in being transcended.

In a very beautiful essay by Josef Piper called "The Negative Element in the Philosophy of St Thomas", Piper suggests that it is crucial for our understanding of St Thomas to ascribe due importance to his view of what it means to be a creature. To be a creature is to be a mystery. We cannot understand anything in its ultimate truth. It is God who holds and who is the secret of all that is. And so the mind, as God's creature, like all other creatures, has a mysterious profundity that eludes its own comprehension. And it is from this profundity that the mind has its capacity to transcend itself without contradicting itself. So supernatural illumination, far from swamping the mind, fulfils it and brings it to its own proper perfection.

St Thomas' doctrine of prophecy brings this out. Prophecy, in his view, is a supernatural mode of seeing which proceeds by way of God's own eternal knowledge, but which does not simply bypass man's innate internal faculties. Not even his imagination: St Thomas says that if God wants to give somebody a prophetic vision, then that person must have a good imagination. And if God wants to give a vision to somebody who has not a good imagination, then he will give them a good imagination first. They can't receive the supernatural illumination without the natural basis for it. Man's mind is made for participation in God's own knowledge of himself and of all that he has made. We must, then, allow God to draw us into his own knowledge, through using our own minds, with *all* the faculties that we have, but always in such a way that the mind's capacity for self-transcendance is also activated and realised.

This brings us to the hub of St Thomas' spiritual teaching, which is not, of course, peculiarly his, but which he expounds with unique thoroughness and authority. I refer to the famous principle that grace does not destroy nature, it rather builds on it and elevates it and, indeed, heals it, so that nature becomes really natural. The idea that the supernatural is unnatural, which is implicit very often in the way that we talk, and unfortunately has even crept into some modern translations of the Bible, is completely repugnant to the whole theology of St Thomas. Grace makes nature natural by healing it, and then builds on it and elevates it.

And so, in the view of St Thomas, little can be achieved in the spiritual life by a grim narrowing down of our interests and a ruthless suppression of our talents. As he says—and I think it is a beautiful principle—it is no worship of the creator to despise God's creatures. His vision is so fascinating because it is at once so unitary and yet vastly comprehensive. All things proceed from God and return to him. He is the source both of their one-ness and of their multiplicity. It is for us to allow the truth of God and of things so to impinge on our minds that we can begin to see everything in this light. Faith gives us a share in God's own knowledge of himself and his knowledge of what he has made. And so, if we are to be drawn into God's own knowledge of himself, then we must be prepared to expand our minds to share in the knowledge of all that God has made.

Theology is so crucially important because it educates us in this overall vision which allows us to see how everthing fits in. It is the discipline of seeing everything from God's own point of view. And as such it is an essential exercise of friendship with God. It is, therefore, as St Thomas said, a kind of wisdom, and as such it has a close connection with charity, even though it is not identical with the gift of the Holy Spirit which we also call wisdom. It isn't just mere equivocation to use the same word, wisdom, in each case. St Cyril of Jerusalem even goes so far as to say that our approach to God depends on our view of created things in this world. I don't think St Thomas could go quite as far as that. But I think he would regard with grave suspicion any alleged faith that did not overflow into a transformed view of things. And this means not just a theoretical view of things. It means a view of things which will have practical consequences too. St Thomas takes it as axiomatic that what we do depends on the way that we see things. This is indeed one of the most elementary applications of his principle of the primacy of the intellect.

So, even if our own chief concern is with getting things done, we must still start with the intellect. We must learn to see things God's way, because we are motivated by what we see. If we see things in a way that is not adequately touched by the truth of God's revelation, then, although our behaviour may be externally conformed to the norms of Christian behaviour, it won't actually become real Christian behaviour; at best it will be a rehearsal for Christian behaviour. We cannot simply generate love of God by willing to love God. Somehow we must come to be attracted by God, and that can only come about through some rudimentary kind of vision of God. That rudimentary vision is faith. And that vision must then be cherished and matured by thought and study, under the constant impulse of the Holy Spirit, who with all his gifts dwells in those who are in a state of grace.

It is indeed God who creates love for himself in us. But he does so in a way that is entirely in accordance with the nature he has given us. God does not force our wills to himself; he woos them. He does this by showing himself in his goodness, in his attractiveness, in all kinds of different ways. But, according to St Thomas, all of those involve creatures, all involve our actual seeing of the things of this world which God uses to disclose himself.

So faith, reflection on faith, the transformation of our vision, which is really what theology is all about, are the essential way in which we let God woo us, so that we can learn what it means to love him.

We have, in our modern world, become rather sceptical

about the role of thinking in our lives. Ideas seem rather too immaterial to matter very much. We've become quite capable of thinking something through to an overwhelmingly certain conclusion, without feeling in the slightest bit obliged to act on that conclusion.

We are quite right to think that our ideas are too immaterial. Because our ideas are precisely immaterial in a way that they shouldn't be. St Thomas is very clear that man is not just an immaterial creature, and that therefore man's ideas are not just immaterial. One of the things that struck his contemporaries was his teaching that man is a single being, a whole. After his death there was a heated controversy as to how many souls man has. What it was all about was whether there is one single vital principle in man, or whether there are several. St Thomas insists that there is one, and that means that man's intellectual life and his spiritual life are not disconnected from his digestion, and indeed from the whole range of bodily, sensual, subconscious processes that go on, even that vital force that makes our toe-nails grow is not totally separate from our spiritual life. Man is a single being, but not a simple one. Man has something in common with the angels, but he also has quite a lot in common with the zoo. And it is both the angel and the zoo in him that must be involved in our relationships with God.

The harmonious ordering of all these bits and pieces that go to make up man is the job of asceticism and morals, and the second part of St Thomas' *Summa* is one of the great masterpieces of ascetic and moral teaching. In it he works out, in great detail, his fundamental teaching that man's return to God, unlike that of the non-intellectual creatures, is characterised by freedom and an intrinsic though caused self-activation. But man's freedom is not an absolute vacuous kind of freedom in which he might like to think he can determine himself in any way he pleases. His freedom is the freedom to be that creature which God has created, his

freedom to be himself. And the other name for that is
humility, which St Thomas defines as the virtue which
teaches a man how to contain himself within his own limits,
not to be bigger or smaller than he is. Humility is the virtue
that recognises that we receive ourselves as free beings,
precisely as creatures of God. We shall hopelessly misunder-
stand ourselves unless we accept that the roots of our freedom lie deep in the mystery of God's creative mind. We
must, in fact, see ourselves rightly. It keeps coming back to
the transformation of our vision, which is fundamental to
the whole ascetical and moral enterprise.

The whole way through, we find an intimate interplay
between natural and supernatural, between vision and
moral endeavour. And over-arching the whole is wisdom.

In St Thomas's view the gift of wisdom is particularly
connected with charity. This again brings us back to the
primacy of intellect. Charity is the essential virtue because
it sets everything in order. Charity sees God as being
supreme, the centre, and values him as the centre. So all our
virtues or activities or interests derive their value from him,
and they find their proper place because charity orders all
of them. It is charity, our interest in God, our fascination
by God, that relativises everything else, and so gives us the
detachment which frees us from self-will and self-interest
which would otherwise blind us. It frees us to be realistic
and objective. Our behaviour depends, then, on our way of
seeing things. But it also feeds back into a way of seeing
things, because it brings us back to our vision of God. St
Thomas is insistent that contemplation is the goal of life,
and moral virtues and asceticism are necessary only because
they prepare us for contemplation. They make us truly
human so that we can be truly filled with the Holy Spirit,
so that we can learn how to rest in sheer contentment in
the vision of God.

I think we can give this a more humane content than
appears at first sight if we take up St Thomas' doctrine of

friendship. For him, friendship is the best word to describe our love for God. He warns us that there are a variety of accidental kinds of friendship that really are not, in the last analysis, friendships, because they do not reach through to the person whom we profess to love. There's a kind of friendship that arises when somebody is useful to us. But what we're really making friends with is the person's usefulness; we're making friends with his bank balance, not with him!

There is another kind of accidental friendship that can arise, the kind that arises when somebody is pleasant, when we enjoy being with him or her. Again, what we are really making friends with is our own enjoyment.

This brings us back to the kind of romantic love that de Rougement exposed. It's love that never really reaches through to someone else. It's love that is concerned only with one's own experience. But true friendship, for St Thomas, consists of *benevolentia*, of wishing somebody well, which is not to be confused with altruism. It isn't necessarily "doing good things" for other people, which after all can be really an impertinence, and at the very least requires that the other person should be in some way at least lower than we. Friendship is between equals, St Thomas says. And so, it would almost seem that it actually excludes altruism, because we are equals and so we are not doing good to each other, we are simply appreciating the good that the other has. Of course this may involve, incidentally, all the other things. Our friend may be useful to us and please God he will be pleasant to us, at least sometimes. And we may be able to help each other in all kinds of ways. But the essence of it is an appreciation of the good that is the other's.

If we apply this to God, surely that brings us straight back to the primacy of the intellect. Our love of God does not consist in enjoying what we can get out of him. It means appreciating his own goodness as it concerns him, not as it concerns us. There is a detachment that must be there if this friendship is to be real. And so the language of passionate love—hugging and all this kind of thing, although it is obviously well vouched for by scripture—could be misleading. The language of contemplation, of seeing, of knowing, does bring out more clearly this element of appreciation.

St Thomas, then, is inviting us to become the kind of people who become capable of radical appreciation of the goodness of God in itself. This means a real emptying out of ourselves, getting beyond all grasping.

But this does not mean that we must simply quench ourselves. He has a lovely phrase in which he says that we should not be put off by our own perfections. He raises the question whether being good at something is a hindrance to devotion. He says no. What we must learn to do is to subject all our perfections to God. And this means allowing all the faculties God has given us to develop, allowing our interests to lead us to endeavour all kinds of things. But always with the context of a supreme concern for God.

If we come to appreciate God supremely for himself, then this will relativise, and in so doing will also validate, all our other aspirations, interests, concerns, powers. It means accepting radically that we are creatures so that all that we are is centred on God. This means that we shouldn't be afraid of being good at sums, good at mending bicycles, good at social work. We shouldn't think that we have to be humble and pretend not to be good at things, that we should try to chop bits off ourselves. It means that our vision of everything should be big enough to contain all other excellencies, so that they actually nourish our devotion and make us more fascinated by God because we see all these things as flowing from him.

St Thomas does not actually connect this with the Eucharist, but I think it is interesting to consider how close this is to what modern research has disclosed to be one of the basic roots of Eucharistic piety: that the Eucharist is the development of the Jewish style of prayer known as the blessing of God. It takes everything in creation and salvation history as the occasion to bless God for himself. Surely it is not accidental that Thomas, who was so devoted to the Eucharist, should have this wonderful all-encompassing vision which can reach out into the whole created order and find in it the occasion to bless God, to appreciate God for what he is.

This gives a new twist to a principle that he takes from Aristotle: that man is a nosey animal, that man wants to know. For Aristotle, man wants to know, he wonders. Wondering makes him take things to bits so that he can find out how things work, and when he finds how they work, that's the end of it, he stops wondering, now he knows.

But for St Thomas it's much more mysterious than that because, as he says, the intellect can penetrate to the very essence of a thing. But the essential principles of things are not known to us. The intellect can penetrate to the very essence of a thing precisely because it can penetrate to the mysteriousness of things. Really grasping what something is, is to grasp it as God's creature. So the more we know, the more we explore things, the more we will discover the mystery of God at the heart of everything.

His doctrine of language has the same consequences. We start by using the word "good", for instance, in very ordinary ways. We talk about a good meal, a good clock, a good neighbour, and it's all very ordinary. Then we work our way up the analogical ladder and start calling God good. But then the whole thing turns inside out because we then discover that it is God who is the measure of goodness. So then we want to come down again, and everything then becomes mysterious because now, if our clock is good, it's because, in some mysterious way, it has a relationship with the goodness of God. There is an elusiveness that is discovered at the heart of everything. The more we look at things, the more they lead us into the mystery of God.

This ties in with St Thomas' own experience. Towards the end of his life, as we know, he had a very mysterious, enigmatic experience. The result was that he declared to his friend Reginald that he just could not go on writing any longer, and all that he had written was just "straw" in comparison with what he had seen. He was not repudiating theology as if it had just been a waste of time. He was saying that he had now reached that stage of theology in which he could no longer go on writing and talking because he had found that to which all his writing and thinking and talking had pointed. He had himself taught about rapture, in which God can bring man, on occasion, to a clarity of vision that is not normally granted to us still on earth. And surely Thomas is saying, in effect, that he has discovered that such rapture is the fulfilment of theology. It is not the job of theology to "tame" God, to make God subject to our neat little schemes. It is the job of theology to bring our minds gradually to sufficient maturity for them to be capable of the mystery of God. Even in this life it may occur that a mind which is so matured, either by the tedious labour of the human intellect working things out, or by the supernatural operations of God's grace, or more probably through a mixture of the two, can sometimes reach such a point, comes so close to the mystery, that it is flooded with a contentment which just silences it.

For St Thomas there is no real dichotomy between our religious activities and the rest of our lives. We know very well that he was capable of so far forgetting himself, because of his concentration on God, that even when he was dining with the King he would get absorbed in working out the implications of certain theological problems. We also know that even when he was engaged in very abstruse and cerebral theology, he would resort to prayer when he got "stuck". His whole life was a life lived in friendship with God, so that whatever he was doing was foremost in his mind. Study for him was meditation. What we can learn from him is that our whole life must be involved in our spiritual life. We can also learn from him to allow God to attract each one of us in the way that particularly suits the temperament that God has given to us, the way that pleases God's own infinite and inventive freedom.

So we should be confident that all that goes on in our lives, all our achievements, all our perfections if we are lucky enough to have any, provided they are subjected to God, will actually foster the spirit of devotion and prayerfulness.

Thomas Aquinas and prayer

St Thomas' discussion of prayer is the longest question in the *Summa*: it runs to seventeen articles. In some ways it is disappointing—I think one must be frank about that. For instance, he does not discuss at all, in connection with prayer, some of the things that we would normally understand as part of one's life of prayer. There are certain whole areas of prayer that he doesn't seem to know about, on which one would love to have his comments; in particular, one would love to know what he would have made of the Jesus prayer.

Also, and perhaps most serious, he doesn't really treat of prayer in its supernatural context. He treats of it as a part of religion, which is a virtue attached to justice! It is a long way away from his treatment of the sacraments. It's a long way from his treatment of the more evidently supernatural phenomena that may turn up in one's life. He is treating it, therefore, strictly as one of the human things that we can arrange. And quite a lot of the things that might interest us about prayer don't come in.

But the seventeen articles do raise a lot of extremely fascinating and very helpful points.

He situates prayer in the context of the virtue of religion, and that is itself situated in the context of justice. Therefore for St Thomas the concept of order is going to be very important: getting things in the right order, giving people what is their due. Religion is particularly important for him. Indeed, he says it is the most important of all the moral virtues—that is to say, the virtues that are not form-

ally supernatural, like the three theological virtues—because
it is the virtue of religion which situates all our activities
with reference to the worship of God.

Again, one would have liked him to connect this with
the Eucharist much more explicitly than he does. It is clearly there but he never quite says so: that the way in which
all our acts are ordered to the worship of God does actually
centre on the Eucharist. The Second Vatican Council does
say it explicitly, and I'm sure Thomas would agree whole-
heartedly.

We must see everything in the light of the centrality of
God. We must act accordingly. And the most direct way of
responding to the centrality of God is worship. For St
Thomas all kinds of things are involved in this. Basically
there are two aspects, an inner and an outer. The outer is
important because we have bodies and we need bodily
worship. The inner is obviously very important, that we
must be involved with our whole human person in worship.
This involves our will and our mind. The involvement of the
will in religion comes under the head of devotion. In this
regard there is one peripheral point of his worth mentioning:
that it is part of a full human life that we should enjoy worship, that we should enjoy the things that pertain to
religious life.

Reading between the lines one gets the impression that
he thoroughly enjoyed all that goes with being Catholic. He
enjoyed lighting candles. He enjoyed using the kind of
bread that the Church uses for Mass. Sometimes we feel
that our worship ought to be very spiritual, and perhaps
don't fully appreciate this dimension of enjoying the things
that pertain to cult, to the expression of worship.

Having dealt with devotion briefly, he launches out into
this great long question on prayer. And the first article may
surprise us. He asks whether prayer is an act of the cogni-
tive or appetitive powers. And he tells us that prayer is not
directly to do with the will, with wanting. It is to do with

the mind. The mind must come to see that God is at the centre of everything. And this will have very profound implications for our approach to our own desires. St Thomas certainly knows that desire is involved in prayer; there must be a want there before the question of prayer arises at all. But mere wanting of itself does not constitute prayer. Prayer is the interpreter of desire.

Now there are several things involved in this. Granted that there is a desire, first we must look to see whether it is a legitimate and proper desire. Prayer is asking God for things that are fitting.

This in itself has two parts. First of all, is it something that is in principle legitimate to want? Secondly, granting that the desire is proper in principle the question arises as to whether our wanting is itself proper, because we can want something that is in principle in order but want it in a way that is disordered. There is nothing in the Gospel to forbid the use of lollipops (proper in principle), but lollipops should only be a relatively small part of one's life (we could have an inordinate desire for them).

So there must be the judgment that one is going to back one's desire. Then there enters a totally different kind of mental activity: how do we set about getting a lollipop? Prayer is the interpreter of desire. It arises from the acknowledgement that God is himself the source of all that might be given to us. It involves the judgment that the best way to get what we want would be to go straight to the top.

St Thomas knows that God is the most basic cause of everything. But secondary causes are the way by which he normally works. So the interpretation of desire into prayer means recognising that God is the ultimate source of all good.

This does have practical consequences. If our friendship with God is to become an outgoing reality in our lives, then surely a very important part of the raw material is going to be precisely our desires. Because as one goes through life one is reacting, left, right and centre. And nearly always one's reactions involve some kind of desire. It may be only a very small desire, and maybe it won't always appear on the surface as desire; we may be more conscious of annoyance, for instance, but annoyance really means the desire that somebody or something will go away.

If we get into the way of systematically interpreting all our desires in the light of the centrality of God, then surely, without even realising it, we are going to draw our whole lives into a relationship with God. More and more we will find that we actually turn even trivial things into a conversation with God. And in so doing a kind of structure will come into it. We simply can't go on saying all day long to God, when people are annoying us, I wish all these people would go home. If one shares one's thoughts and one's feelings with God, inevitably one is challenged by God's own attitudes so that they will come to be formed by God. And then, more and more, one will find that, out of one's desires and reactions, more and more instinctively, comes a kind of warmth towards God, whether it be the warmth that comes when you desperately need help, or whether it be the kind of warmth that comes just from having a little joke with God.

All this, of course, comes from seeing things in a certain kind of way, in such a way that one can be open to God. And that means interpreting one's experience.

The next question is whether it is appropriate to pray. St Thomas discusses the three errors which, he says, have tended to arise in connection with prayer. And the first of these is that all that goes on in the world is quite independent of God. Things are not ruled by God's providence, so there's no point at all in telling God about it.

The second error is the opposite: that everything is absolutely fixed, and is going to come about whatever we do, so there is no particular point in telling God about it.

The third error is that of supposing that God actually

changes his mind, that God does not know what he is going
to do until someone comes along and tells him what to do.

He says none of these will do. He gives us a very important theoretical principle that, again, has very real practical
consequences for prayer. He says we must take it as a
matter of faith that God's will does not depend on us.
God's will is fixed and that is that. But God's will involves
not only what he wants to achieve but also the way in
which he wishes to achieve it. It involves, therefore, all the
various secondary causes that God may choose to involve in
the working out of his will. And prayer is one such secondary cause.

So, to deal with the third objection, it isn't as though
God were just sitting there scratching his head and thinking,
what should we do about this or that? God knows perfectly
well what it is he proposes to achieve. And within that, he
proposes to achieve certain things by means of certain
people praying. So our prayer is not outside God's will, it is
inside God's will; our prayer is itself willed by God as a
means to the end willed by God.

This of course also deals with the objection that it's all
fixed and so there's no point in telling God what you think.
The prayer isn't just telling God what you think. It is seeking to realise a role that God has allocated to one in his own
infinite freedom. God has willed that such and such should
come about through our prayers, and he wants us to be
involved like that in the working out of his will. God does
not just want us to be passive to the things he does; he
wants us to be cooperators with him in his work, and our
praying is one of the ways in which he invites us to share
with him in bringing about what he wants. His will is basic;
that comes before anything else. But it involves an invitation
to us to enter sympathetically into his will.

And then, of course, we must realise that absolutely
everything is ruled by divine providence. This has a lot of
very important practical consequences. One is that we must

ask ourselves sometimes how far we do really believe that everything is subject to God's providence. As we go through life, most of us, very comfortably, are part-time Christians because we have not taken to heart the doctrinal principle that God really is the lord of all. So we just don't see the connections between God and many of the things that arise in our lives. Surely here is something that we should seek from God: to have a faith that grows and becomes more and more all-encompassing, so that more and more things do actually become potential matter for prayer.

And then, how often we want to sit back and say to God, you get on with it. We can't really be bothered to involve ourselves more actively in God's will. And in connection with prayer we have actually made a doctrine out of this. We have said that the most perfect kir.d of prayer is to say, thy will be done, as if to sign a blank cheque and to give it to God and to forget about it.

But St Thomas, if he is right, is at least making it less possible for us to do that. If we are to be actually involved in the working out of God's will, which is to bring about specific ends, then we must be prepared in principle to let God reveal to us his specific ends. We should not approach prayer as if it were just a matter of telling God what we want, and then leaving it in his hands. We must begin by placing ourselves within his will and trying to become sensitive to his will, and then pray within his will.

Article five of the *Summa* develops this very point: whether we should pray for anything in particular. The case against is very strong. It would seem that we shouldn't pray for anything in particular because as St John Damascene says, prayer is asking God for things that are fitting. So it is useless to pray for things that are not fitting. And then he refers to St James: you ask and you do not receive because you ask badly. But—and here he quotes St Paul—we do not know what we should pray for as we ought. QED—therefore we should not ask for anything in particular in our prayer! And then there is another little point: that telling God what we think would really seem to be turning things upside down, that we should not be bending his will to us, that we should be bending our will to his.

In dealing with this St Thomas refers back to a Roman historian talking about Socrates saying that we should ask the immortal gods for nothing except that they should grant us good things, because they know what is good for each one and we often ask for the very things that we would be much better without.

St Thomas says there's a certain amount of truth in that, at least as far as those things are concerned which could get us into trouble. For instance, having a lot of money can be very nice; but it can be dangerous. But there are certain things which can't go wrong, he says. And he quotes two prayers from the Bible. "Show us your face and we shall be saved." It's difficult to see what could go wrong with that. And again: "Lead me in the way of your commands." It's difficult to see what could go wrong with that, an utterly safe thing to pray for. And then, of course, the Lord's Prayer itself gives us very specific petitions.

Should one, then, just stick to things that are absolutely safe like that?

It is not quite as simple as that. Answering what seems like an insuperable difficulty, St Thomas says it's true that a man by himself doesn't know what he ought to pray for. But he quotes from *Romans*: "The Spirit helps our weakness. And he inspires us with holy desires, and so makes us pray rightly." And this is why the Lord says that "true worshippers must worship in spirit and in truth." It is a very interesting use of that particular text. Left to ourselves we wouldn't know what to ask for. If that were all that had to be said about it, then we should just stick to the things that are absolutely safe. But we're not left to ourselves. As Christians we have received the Holy Spirit who makes us worshippers in spirit and in truth, so that we can pray in the Holy Spirit and in the truth. He doesn't comment any further on that. But surely that means that there is a kind of accuracy that should be involved in prayer. There's a prayer that is the right prayer, a prayer that in principle we should be able to recognise.

But I think it is very important that St Thomas connects this with the Holy Spirit inspiring us with holy desires. Because you can't pray for what you don't want. It's no good just having hypothetical desires, thinking that what you ought to be praying for is the virtue of humility if, frankly, you don't want to be humble, if you're perfectly happy being conceited. What the Holy Spirit will do is make you slightly less happy; he will begin to inspire a holy desire, and from that holy desire will come the holy prayer.

Sometimes we like to deceive ourselves that we are being terribly holy because we are ignoring all the things that we really want and are giving ourselves generously to what we know to be the will of God, so that we can have the satisfaction of being martyrs, so that we can feel superior. It is basic to St Thomas' whole approach to the Christian life that this attitude is not good enough. The test of real virtue is whether we are enjoying it. The test of whether we are really doing God's will or not is whether at the same time we are doing our own will. The most important thing isn't just that we do it but that we want to do it. The conversion of one's wanting is the basic thing, and from that behaviour will flow. So St Thomas is forbidding us that handy kind of schizophrenia where we can admire ourselves doing the will of God.

The next point that St Thomas raises is whether we should ask for temporal things when we pray. Unfortunately he doesn't connect this any further with his principle about our praying within God's will. But he makes a very sensible observation—which he takes from St Augustine— that whatever it is lawful to desire it is lawful to pray for. And it is lawful to desire temporal things; indeed, it is not only lawful, it is an integral part of our being human. That's the way God has made us—the zoo bit of us!

The trouble is that we tend to get things out of their proper perspective, so that we have an exaggerated commitment to things that are less important, and an inadequate commitment to the things that are more important. But we don't solve that by simply writing off prayer for temporal things. So we must learn again how to desire rightly. This is the chief point he makes in his commentary on the Lord's Prayer: that it contains, at least implicitly, all the things that we can legitimately desire, and it contains them in the right order.

There are also some practical points that St Thomas raises. Granted that we are seeking to have our desires transformed by the Holy Spirit so that our prayers will be accurate, how do we actually set about it? How does prayer work?

There are three immensely practical questions here. First of all whether our prayer must be vocal. Secondly, whether it is necessary for prayer that we be paying attention to what we are saying. Thirdly, whether we should go on for a long time, or not.

With regard to the first, should prayer be vocal, he says, apparently not, because God listens to the heart, so there is no point in saying our prayers out loud. In prayer it is the mind of man that ascends to God, and the mind is distracted by chatter. And also, prayers should be offered to God secretly: "Enter into your chamber and close the door." And if you start praying out loud, then you're not praying secretly.

He very reasonably points out that we sometimes pray together, and then obviously the prayer has to be out loud; we wouldn't otherwise know when to say "Amen", for example. But when we're praying privately, he says we don't *have to* pray out loud but there are various reasons why it might be considered appropriate sometimes. First of all, it might be "to excite one's inner devotion", because often through external signs, whether in the form of gestures or speaking, the mind of man is stirred. So one begins by praying with the body, we pray in gesture, like making the sign of the cross, and we then say our prayers out loud.

After all, this is simply to take our own humanity seriously, that that's the kind of creature we are. If we are talking to God, then our normal human way to talk is to talk. And generally we find it easier to concentrate on our talking, at least sometimes, when we are actually forming the words and saying them. This is why, in at least one major reform of the Church, one of the things that were insisted on was that priests must say their office, not actually out loud, but moving their lips, and that got into the rubrics and stayed there until a few years ago. This was meant to make sure that one wasn't just drifting through a kind of mental fog.

Then, one owes a debt to God, who has given us a body as well as a soul, and therefore one must worship him with the body as well as the soul. So even if one's heart and one's mind, on occasion, are not the slightest bit interested in one's bodily worship, there still remains a basic validity in bodily worship because the body itself must pray, quite apart from what the heart or mind may be doing. This is not to say that it is wholly satisfactory if we just pray with our body. But it is something. And it is consoling: sometimes we get as far as the sign of the cross and stand there looking at the crucifix, and we can't do anything more—but at least our body is worshipping.

And he makes a typical mediaeval monastic statement: sometimes vocal prayer is joined to one's prayer from a certain overflow from the soul into the body, from vehement affection. As Scripture says, "My heart rejoiced and my tongue jumped for joy." This is something the early Dominicans knew a lot about, because St Dominic prayed with tremendous gusto; he used to wake the brethren up at night with his roaring and bellowing and shouting. They didn't like it, and they wrote into the constitutions that the Novice-Master was to instruct the novices not to roar and bellow when they prayed.

What he is saying is, let's be human. We've got bodies, and it's natural for us to express ourselves with bodies. We don't have to gesticulate when we talk to God, but it's natural to do so, and if we want to gesticulate, let us.

This raises the question of distractions, and it does arise particularly in connection with vocal prayer. Because if our mind is held in simple concentration, then there is no problem. But if we're talking externally then we can, in fact, get quite a long way from what we're saying. It would seem at first sight that this would invalidate the prayer. But St Thomas says no. What is necessary for prayer is not attention but intention. This again is very consoling: as long as we are intending to pray, then our prayer will result. If we can actually attend and be fully involved in what is going on, then we are likely to get more of the incidental benefits of prayer; we are more likely to find our hearts and our minds refreshed if they have been involved in our prayers.

Again, this is really a matter of knowing that we are human. The mind of man can't stay up on high for very long. But it's still worth doing. We say our prayers, and our mind will come tagging along every now and then. Lucky the mind that will decide it is worth joining in too.

Should prayer go on for a long time? This is one of those vexed questions and it is very interesting to see how it is raised. The onus is on those who want to say that we should go on for a long time. There was a very insistent monastic tradition that prayer should be frequent and brief. But St Thomas hedges. Formally he argues that one should go on for a long time. But he then says that the essential thing is not the prayer but the charity that underlies the prayer; it is one's desire for God that should go on a long

time, should go on the whole time, in fact. In that sense
one's prayer should go on without ceasing.

But the actual praying as a specific activity has no built-
in time consideration at all. He refers back to the monastic
tradition of frequent and very brief prayer. But he doesn't
simply take it up as if that settled the matter. He is saying,
again, let's be human, let's take seriously the kind of
creatures that we are. And as long as our prayer is express-
ive of devotion, of the fervour of our inner desire, then by
all means let the prayer go on. We don't have to stop it just
to satisfy some monastic rubric. But "when you can't go on
without tedium, then you should not prolong your prayer
any further". What we are trying to achieve is an overall
state of friendship with God in which the whole of our life
will be lived in union with him. We are not going to build
up a friendly feeling for God if a large part of our experience of God is one of being bored by him. If the transformation of one's vision is going on as it should be, in St
Thomas' view, one should become less bored by God and
therefore more likely to be able to spend more time with
him. But on the other hand, that time spent with him
won't necessarily be in prayer, because anything that one
does can be time spent with him.

Simon Tugwell, OP

4　St Teresa

Her life, times and spirituality

The holy and truly liberated woman known as the great Teresa was born in 1515 in Avila, a hill-town in central Spain. It helps to place her in her time to recall that in the year of her birth Martin Luther, still an exemplary Augustinian and university professor, was in his early thirties; two years were to elapse before he burst upon the European and religious scene. Ignatius Loyola, his four years' soldiering and subsequent conversion lying ahead, was then a courtier in his early twenties. Three young monarchs, rivals, Henry VIII, Francis I and the Emperor Charles V, were moving on to absolute power.

Spain was on the crest of the wave, on her way to becoming the first power in Europe and the known world. Her Emperor was overlord not only of Spain and the new Spain across the Atlantic, but had inherited from his Hapsburg father and grandfather Germany, the Netherlands and Austria, with rich slices of France, Italy and the north African coast. It was a time not unlike our own, a time of unprecedented, rapid and continuous change.

To return to Teresa—recent research on the saint's ancestry brought an interesting fact to light. Her grandfather, her father's father, was a Jew, one of a wealthy Jewish family in the wealthy city of Toledo. Their prosperity was mainly due to an extensive silk trade, based on the silkworms reared on their mulberry farms.

At that pre-Inquisition period intermarriage between

Jews and Christians was fairly common in certain circles in
Spain. The nobles envied the Jews their wealth; the Jews
envied the power and prestige of the nobility. Jews marry-
ing Christians accepted baptism as a required formality;
these nominal Christians were called *conversos* and often,
when the marriage ceremony was over, they returned to the
faith of Abraham, Isaac and Jacob.

Teresa's grandfather was a *converso* who had married the
daughter of a Spanish grandee and afterwards, to the
scandal of his in-laws, reverted to Judaism. But his silks,
damasks and cloth-of-gold were so excellent that most
Spanish bishops ordered their vestments from him; he was
appointed supplier of state robes to royalty and, in return,
was conferred with the title of *hidalgo* or minor nobleman.
Later, when the courts of the Inquisition were set up in
Toledo, he did not wait to be accused or arrested but went
before the tribunal, confessed his lapse, promised future
fidelity to the Christian faith and did the imposed penance.
For seven Fridays he donned the garment of shame, the
yellow *san-benito*, and walked in the public procession of
the reconciled through the city streets.

This adverse publicity was bad for business, but reverses
only proved the man's mettle. He moved to Avila, a walled
city with eighty-eight towers—still standing today as they
did in his time. Prosperity followed him to that town on
the plain of Castile. He married his sons to the first families
there and, although his Jewish blood and his brush with the
Inquisition became known in strictly orthodox Avila, he
was popular and on his death given the honour of a tomb in
the cathedral. None of his seven sons inherited his drive, his
business sense, his resolute character, his open, attractive
manner, his greatness of heart. These qualities skipped a
generation to appear in his grand-daughter, Teresa.

Many years later Teresa, speaking of how the soul
becomes united to God in prayer, took the silkworm on the
mulberry leaves for comparison. The sun, stirring the larvae

to life and action, she compared to the light and fire of the
Holy Spirit; the silkworm, spinning its silken thread until it
is entirely enclosed in a cocoon, to the soul praying until its
life becomes hidden with Christ in God; it emerges like the
butterfly, so transformed by this unitive prayer that it is
ceaselessly active, ready to spend itself, to suffer, to die for
God. She admits that she never saw a silkworm or a mulberry tree, but someone must have told the child Teresa
about the mulberry farms in Toledo and the silkworms that
founded the fortunes of the grandfather she never knew.

Teresa was the third child of her father's second marriage.
Her mother, a delicate, self-effacing woman, was fond of
reading tales of chivalry, the sixteenth-century equivalent
of today's novelettes; they were then very popular in Spain,
St Ignatius tells us that he spent hours reading them. But
Teresa's religious training was not neglected; her mother
taught her her prayers and how to say the rosary; the child
shared her mother's love for our Lady; at an early age she
learned to read and was given simple lives of the saints. Her
mother's books all ended with the words "and they lived
happily ever after"; eternal happiness was a thought that
fascinated little Teresa; she would repeat the words *forever
and forever and forever* over and over.

Reading of Franciscans martyred by African Moors in
the time of St Francis, Teresa decided that they had made a
good bargain in exchanging cruel but brief torments for un-
ending bliss. So she persuaded the brother nearest herself in
age to run away with her "to the land of the Moors" which
she probably thought was a few miles away across the plain;
there they would be beheaded and go straight to heaven—
instant salvation. They were missed, searched for, found
and fetched home; the grown-ups concluded, rightly, that
Teresa was the planner of the escapade. That formidable
thought, the endlessness of eternity, the brevity and fleeting nature of human life, was to remain with her always.
She sums it up for her nuns:

"Life is but a bad night in a wretched inn."

As she grew older she developed a taste for the escapist reading her mother enjoyed and could not bear to be without a new book. Her father, austere, upright, kind and good to the poor, had a library of scholarly and devotional books; he did not approve of frivolous reading, so there was a rush to hide the romances when his step was heard. Like other *hidalgos* he lived beyond his means, with many servants in the Avila house and on their country estate, but he had not his father's head for business and was to die in debt.

When Teresa was thirteen her mother died, leaving an infant girl; there were also an older step-sister and several brothers. Teresa, a good chess-player, played with and often checkmated her father. She was pretty, gay, and fond of jewellery and perfume; one who knew her in her early teens said that she liked to set off the pallor of her skin and her dark hair by wearing orange-coloured dresses banded with black velvet. Her father, always strict about those admitted to his home, could not shut the door on relatives who came after his wife's death to console the bereaved family. One older cousin, a girl disapproved of by Teresa's mother, was constantly in the house and a bad influence on the younger girl.

Other cousins, boys, came too and a teenage romance between Teresa and one of these was encouraged and played up by the servants. Looking back from the heights of sanctity at this episode, which was probably harmless enough, Teresa always deplored it, but admitted that if she held back from sin it was simply for the sake of the family honour; she could not or would not bring shame on her father and brothers.

In 1531 the Empress came to Avila bringing her son, the small boy whom history was to know as Philip II. She stayed for the summer and there were tournaments, bull-fights and other festivities which the sixteen-year-old Teresa enjoyed. Her step-sister was now married and her father decided that his vivacious second daughter should go as a boarder to a local convent school. Teresa wept, not because she was leaving home or disliked the idea of school, but because she thought that everyone in Avila knew of her indiscreet romance and that she was being sent to school as a result of that indiscretion. She soon settled down and liked her teachers, Augustinian nuns. She asked one nun what had prompted her to enter religion and got the reply, "The Gospel text, *Many are called but few are chosen.*" But Teresa felt no inclination to follow her example.

After eighteen months at school she became seriously ill and her father thought that a stay at her step-sister's home in the country would benefit her. On the way there she stayed with an uncle, Pedro, a devout man fond of reading spiritual books. His favourites were the letters of St Jerome, and St Gregory the Great's commentary on the Book of Job. He asked Teresa to read to him, which she did "because," she says, "I always wanted to please people, so as to be liked by them".

As she read, eternity again loomed ahead; she told herself, "If I died of the sickness I might end up in hell. . . Perhaps the religious life is the safest and best; and since I cannot persuade myself to enter I must force myself to do so." Not a very lofty motive, to say the least of it. "So," she continues, "I read St Gregory on Job to help me to bear the sickness with patience, and I read St Jerome to encourage myself to enter." She may have read Jerome's letter to Heliodorus with its stern questions: *Why are you, a Christian, so lacking in spirit? What are you doing in the world?*

She recovered, came home, but did not return to school. The brothers were leaving, one by one, to seek their fortunes in the Indies. She asked her father's permission to become a nun: after his death, not before, was the answer. For two years she kept asking and he kept refusing. Finally, on All Souls' morning 1535 she slipped out as though going to early Mass, went straight to the Carmelite convent of the

Incarnation where a friend of hers was a nun, and was admitted. Teresa was then a few months short of her twenty-first birthday; she tells us that she had to do such violence to herself to take the step that she felt as though every bone in her body was being wrenched apart.

The Incarnation convent had been originally founded as a residence by a group of pious ladies who wished to live together, rather like the *béguines* in Flemish cities prior to Vatican II. Twenty years before Teresa's entry they decided to form a religious community and take vows; they adopted the mitigated or mild form of the Carmelite rule. There was no enclosure, no common refectory; nuns whose families were wealthy had suites of rooms and were provided with food by their relatives; others slept in dormitories and depended on alms or their sisters in religion for food. As there were 180 nuns in the community in 1535, many of them poor, they were encouraged to visit and remain with their families for indefinite periods—especially when food was scarce. So that alms might be forthcoming, the parlours were always open and guests made welcome.

When Teresa's father found that his daugher had taken the law into her own hands he made the best of things and provided handsomely for her. She had a bedroom, a guest room, a kitchen and a little oratory; her father settled an income on her, gave her material for mantles, habits and coifs, two beds with bed-coverings; he supplied her with wheat and barley, a sheepskin cloak, veils "and the books which are usually given to nuns". He also pledged himself to give a grand reception to the entire community on her reception and profession day.

Though the rule was not strictly observed, things were not as relaxed as some writers lead us to believe. The novitiate was testing; fasting, silence, Office sung in choir, vocal prayer and bodily penance were usual. Teresa was a fervent novice but she had no illusions about herself. She describes herself as a novice:

Though I liked everything that had to do with religious life, I could not bear anything that made me
look ridiculous. I delighted in being thought well of
(*don't we all?*). I knew very little of the Office or of
what I ought to do in choir or how to behave, so I
was careless and caught up in other vanities. Other
novices could have taught me, but I did not ask
them lest they become aware of how little I knew...
I was also bad at singing and I felt this very much,
not for my shortcomings in the sight of the Lord,
but because of all the nuns listening to me. . . When
I ceased caring whether my ignorance were known
or not, I improved.

Profession day came and her father excelled himself, giving
a splendid banquet and presenting a new linen coif to each
of the 180 nuns. Soon afterwards Teresa's health declined;
she suffered heart attacks, fainting fits, lost appetite and
grew thin and weak. The Avila doctors failed to find a
remedy. As enclosure was not obligatory her father arranged
for herself and another nun to go to a *curandera*, a wise
woman with a cure, who lived fifty miles away. Again there
was a stop at Uncle Pedro's who presented her with a book,
Osuna's *Third Spiritual Alphabet*; it dealt with the recollection needed for prayer, a prayer new to Teresa—prayer of
the mind and heart.

In spring the cure began, but it proved worse than the
illness. The remedies were so drastic that the patient
suffered agonies, steadily disimproved and was finally taken
home to die. In August she lapsed into a coma that lasted
four days; her grave was dug at the Incarnation and she
would have been buried alive only that her father insisted
she was still living. She regained consciousness, but her
sufferings continued. She was carried back to her convent
and was a complete invalid for eight months when she
could crawl about on hands and knees; for the next two
years and more she was a semi-invalid and she was to have
wretched health for the rest of her life.

Thanks to Uncle Pedro's spiritual A-B-C she trained herself to recollection, and began to practise the prayer it recommended, "a friendly and familiar conversation with God", but conversion was still in the future. She was now in her late twenties, and as she got stronger her natural vivacity returned; she frequented the parlours, becoming the most popular nun there. Through her, alms and gifts came in abundance, so she was encouraged to entertain the ladies and gallants of Avila who brought in all the news of the day. But she was divided against herself. She says:

> In the midst of worldly pleasures I was distressed by the thought of what I owed to God; and when I was with God I grew restless because the world drew me ... Often I spent the hour of prayer waiting for the clock to strike... and I would rather do any penance than recollect myself in order to pray.

This see-sawing continued for the next seven years. She got warnings, some of them heaven-sent and rather frightening. Once she gave up prayer for a long period. She saw her dearly-loved father die; his death was holy, his last words a reminder of the brevity of life. Again the thought of eternity, of how all things pass, gripped her. She told the Dominican who attended her father of her dissatisfaction with her mediocre life. He advised her to resume prayer and to receive Holy Communion once a fortnight—fairly frequent, even for a nun, in that time. She began to pray again and read, this time a *Life of Christ* by Ludolph of Saxony, a work which sent her to read the Scriptures. At this period, too, she read *The Confessions of St Augustine*. In his postponement of conversion she saw her own.

For ten more years she dallied, between two worlds so to speak; but she prayed. Later she made the wise observation,

> One should not wait until one is perfect, or even until one is converted before giving oneself to

prayer... It would be the sad day if we could not draw near to God until we were dead to worldly things. Think of the Magdalen and the Samaritan woman and the woman of Canaan. Were they perfect, or converted, when they approached and found him?

The saying "Life begins at forty" proved true in Teresa's case. She began to see, but not with her bodily eyes, to hear words addressed to her, but not through her sense of hearing; these revelations came during prayer and, though they convinced her, frightened her. She told herself that she was imagining things, that she was deceiving herself. A few years previously, Maddalena de la Cruz, a Poor Clare from Cordoba, had made a shocking disclosure. For twenty years Maddalena had been revered by all as a saint; her prophecies all came true, she had worked miracles. The Empress sent her the Infanta's christening robes to embroider with her holy hands. The Grand Inquisitor, sent to interrogate her, knelt before her and begged her to pray for him. One day the Poor Clare fell ill; thinking that she was dying, she sent for the civil and ecclesiastical authorities and declared upon oath that all her holiness was a sham; she had made a pact with the devil twenty years before and her prophecies and wonder-working were due to his intervention.

Teresa had further cause for alarm. A sect known as the *Alumbrados* had sprung up in southern Spain; they practised the kind of prayer Teresa had adopted and claimed to receive divine illumination in prayer. Some of the *Alumbrados* were orthodox, but others deviated far from the right way; their hysterical devotions, exaggerated penances, their prophecies and, in some cases, their moral excesses drew upon them the attention of the Inquisition. Women were particularly drawn to this sect. Teresa had heard of them:

> Everyone in Avila was talking about some women who had been greatly deluded by Satan; I became

> terrified, experiencing the strange and delightful
> favours granted to me, and which I was utterly
> unable to prevent.

She told her confessor of her experiences; during the
following years she told a whole series of confessors. The
first priests she consulted were not very helpful. They knew
her as the nun in most demand in the parlours, the popular
sister whose witty sayings were repeated all over Avila—
definitely not the kind to receive heavenly favours and revelations; worldly ways were not consistent with holiness.
They assured her that she was being led by a spirit but
certainly not by the Spirit of God. But the visions and locutions continued, and other phenomena which embarrassed
her greatly if they occurred in public. The nuns saw her go
into ecstasy, they saw her enraptured, lifted bodily from
the ground even when they tried to hold her down. Some
sisters hoped that they had not a Maddalena de la Cruz in
their convent.

A visit from Francis Borgia, the one-time Duke who had
become a Jesuit and was yet to be a canonised saint, allayed
her fears somewhat; he told her that he had experiences
similar to those she described to him and assured her that
she was on the right road. A few years later another saint,
Peter of Alcantara, gave her even more reassurance. Peter
belonged to a barefoot, reformed branch of the Franciscan
Order that followed the primitive rule of St Francis. His
penances were truly alarming. Teresa gives us a description
of the saint and his austerities:

> For forty years he slept sitting upright in a cell four
> feet long; for pillow he nailed a block of wood to
> the cell wall. He ate once every three days, some-
> times once a week. "You get quite used to it," he
> told me. . . He looked as though he were made of
> the roots of trees; he seldom lifted his eyes from the
> ground, knew none of his brethren by sight and
> found his way around the friary by following their

footsteps. I found him most affable, easy to speak
to, delightful to listen to, and highly intelligent.

He found in Sister Teresa of Jesus a kindred soul led by
ways with which he was very familiar. He told her of the
reform of his Order and went his way, singing and making
melody as was his custom. (As a matter of fact he died singing. One day the friars were amazed to see him fall on his
knees and begin to sing the psalm *Laetatus sum*: "I rejoiced
when they said to me, 'Let us go into the House of the
Lord.'" Still singing, still on he knees, he died.)

The word Reform was on everyone's lips at this time, for
the Council of Trent, which began in 1545, having seen in
the Protestant Reformation a reaction against the Church's
failure to reform herself, was undertaking a radical reform
from within the Church. The older Orders undertook to
reform themselves, new Orders—Jesuits, Oratorians, Thea-
tines—became the spearhead of the Counter-Reformation.
Teresa knew that Spain's newly-acquired power and afflu-
ence was leading to a decadence that infected the nation,
the clergy, the religious. One wonders did Peter of Alcantara
quote for her the maxim of St Clare of Assisi, *The walls of
poverty are strong*; for poverty now assumed high importance in her eyes—poverty and reform.

The reformed Franciscans had adopted the primitive rule
of St Francis; Teresa began to enquire about the primitive
Carmelite rule, and the Carmelite vocation to be *in* the
world yet not *of* the world; to pray and suffer in silence
and solitude; to intercede for all, but especially for priests;
to be the Moses on the hilltop fighting for the Israelites on
the plain. She found that at least two other nuns shared her
ideas and they discussed what a reformed Carmel should be
like; a few nuns, usually thirteen, in a small poor house
"that would not make a great crash falling down on judgment day"; provision for solitude indoors and out, that
solitude so helpful for prayer.

Suddenly things began to happen. A friend found a little house. Teresa's brother Lorenzo, grown wealthy in the Indies, sent the wherewithal to buy it. But news of the plan leaked out and there was uproar. The city fathers said that Avila had already far too many religious houses, all dependant upon alms; another one would be the last straw. The nuns in the Incarnation accused Teresa of insulting them and of having no love for her community; they could very well have used the money spent on buying a new house. Some said, "Throw sister Teresa into the prison cell." (Sisters who read this, consider yourselves lucky to live in our times! In former days every convent had a prison-cell where flighty or odd or highly-strung or recalcitrant nuns were locked up. And if they showed signs of a nervous breakdown they got the recognised treatment for mental disorders in convents as in society at large until compara-tively recent times—they were given hard blows with a stick!)

Reports that Teresa had been "seeing and hearing things" were bandied about and friends begged her to beware of the Inquisition. Ignatius of Loyola, now with God, had been hauled before it twice and imprisoned at Salamanca. The Archbishop of Toledo, related to princes of the blood, had been jailed for his commentary on a catechism; he remained there until his death eighteen years later. Even Francis Borgia and the Infanta Juana, sister to King Philip, were under suspicion.

Teresa felt somewhat uneasy because a manuscript, her life and method of prayer, which her confessor had ordered her to write, was—very much against her will—being handed around to all and sundry. She bore the abuse, the opposition to the new convent calmly, saying that if the Lord wanted a reformed convent founded it would be founded; it seemed an impossible project but she had been assured in prayer that it would succeed. And so it did. In August 1562 four penniless novices were admitted to St Joseph's Convent, Avila, clothed in rough frieze and given the strict Carmelite rule.

All was lovely and serene, but not for long. Stones were thrown; threats were shouted through the keyhole by citizens who felt that the support of this mushroom convent would fall on them. Teresa, praying before the Blessed Sacrament, was beset by doubts. Had God really wanted her to found this convent? Would she, with her wretched health, be able to look after the four novices? To add to her worries a message came from the Prioress of the Incarnation commanding her to return to her own convent at once. She obeyed, leaving the novices in the care of St Joseph.

Her reception at the Incarnation was not very sisterly. Some asked how she, who for twenty years had failed to observe their mild rule, now thought she could observe the very austere early rule—she who was always in the parlours. Others dismissed her as a notice-box. The Prioress sent for the Carmelite Father-Provincial who reprimanded Teresa, but told her privately that when the tumult in the town died down she could return to St Joseph's. By Christmas, fortified by a Brief a resourceful friend had obtained from Rome, Teresa was back with her novices. There she spent five quiet and happy years, making herself the servant of all, loth to leave her spinning wheel to complete the books her confessor commanded her to write and the instructions on prayer and the Carmelite life she was writing for her nuns. To all appearances the world would hear of her no more.

By this time the Council of Trent was ending and Philip of Spain was asked to promote Church reform in his dominions. When the Carmelite Father-General visited the peninsula the king sent for him and discussed the question. The General visited Avila and was so pleased with St Joseph's that Teresa was commanded to found other houses of the discalced, not only for nuns but also for the Carmelite friars. From that on it was goodbye to peace and tranquillity. The last fifteen years of sister Teresa's life were to be spent traversing the roads and mule-tracks of Spain, in

scorching heat, in bitter cold; during that period she
founded seventeen convents, power-houses of prayer, while
ten houses of the Discalced friars were founded in her lifetime.

She records these journeys in the *Book of the Foundations*, almost a travel diary and meant not only to edify
but to amuse her nuns. For those who have not read the
works of St Teresa, this is the best one to begin with; she
describes people she met, saints and sinners, beggars and
princes. She had interviews with Philip II; she endured the
vagaries of that subject of so many plays, books and films,
the one-eyed Princess of Eboli. The Princess became a
Carmelite the very evening she became a widow, despite the
wailing of her six orphans; she made her own rules, causing
the distraught Prioress to write to the Foundress, "The
Princess is a nun. This house is finished." Teresa changed
the nuns to another town, whereupon the one-eyed lady,
who had left Carmel as hastily as she entered, got embroiled
in high politics and ended up with a life-sentence in a prison
cell.

Teresa tells us how she and the nuns travelled, of their
adventures and misadventures, of bulls being driven in for
the bull-fights, of leaking ferry-boats, rivers in flood that
had to be crossed and filthy inns where muleteers and
soldiers drank and shouted and brawled while the poor
nuns cowered in an adjoining room. Once, in Salamanca on
All Souls' Night, some students were evicted from an inn-
room to make way for Teresa and the timid nun who
accompanied her. "Students are not very tidy people,"
remarks Teresa. The dead bell tolled all night and the other
sister kept peering about, fearing that a student or two
might still be lurking in the shadows. "Mother," she asked,
"what would you do if I died tonight and you were left
alone?" "Sister," came the reply, "I'll think about that
when it happens. Meanwhile let us try to sleep."

This endless journeying took place between Teresa's

fifty-third and sixty-eighth year and her health, never good, was not improved by the hardship. How this ageing, delicate woman accomplished so much in so short a time is amazing; she searched for houses, arranged for their purchase or renting (for which begging letters had to be written to wealthy friends), transacted business with civil and Church authorities, saw to repairs and alterations, interviewed postulants and made time to write to the nuns in the different houses before setting off on another long journey in the jolting, covered-in mulecart. Her letters show her strength of character, her genius for organising, and all the qualities she inherited from her Toledo grandfather; they are often most entertaining.

She writes to one, "You could bribe me with a sardine." Again and again she tells correspondents, "I nearly died laughing." Writing to the young Prioress of a new foundation she says that she is glad the Jesuit Fathers will act as the nuns' confessors and chaplains. She adds, "Be sure and think up lots of questions to ask them. Jesuits like that." In a thank-you note she writes, "Thanks for the orange-flower water and the quinces and the honey; as for the tunny fish, we left it at Malagon, and long may it stay there." She replied to a flatterer, "When I was a girl everyone told me that I was beautiful and I believed them; when I was older they told me I was very intelligent and I believed them; now they tell me that I am a saint, but I have no more illusions."

If asked, Teresa would probably have given the Reform as her most important work. She hardly foresaw that her teaching on prayer, intended only for her confessors and her nuns and a few persons who asked her advice, would be translated into twenty-two languages and run into 1,212 editions. It is pleasant to note that the first translations of her works into English was done by an Irishman, Fr William Malone SJ, in 1611, not quite thirty years after the saint's death.

She accuses herself of being too wordy, too irrelevant, to *leadránach*, in her writing; she says, "I have this awful failing; I never can make myself understood without using torrents of words." It is the hopping of her agile mind from this to that and back again that gives her writing its unique spontaneity and piquancy; she writes as she speaks. One marvels, recalling that she began as a reader of trashy tales and received only eighteen months formal education; she explains things: "Teresa alone can do nothing. Teresa and Almighty God can do much; nothing is impossible to God."

In 1571 her superiors ordered her back to Avila to reform the convent of the Incarnation which had become poor and was reduced to 130 nuns. It was a difficult assignment; not everyone who needs reform welcomes the reform or the reformer. Teresa had been appointed Prioress; some nuns tried to bar the door against her; others shouted her down, but the following year the Father-Visitor was able to make this report:

> There is as much peace and holiness in the Incarnation now as in the houses of the Discalced. I was extraordinarily surprised and encouraged; it all comes from the presence of *La Madre*, The Mother.

Relieved of this post in 1574 she set out again to visit early foundations and make ten new ones, as well as houses of friars. It will be remembered that St John of the Cross was about to join the Carthusians when she won him to the Reform. For the next eight years persecutions and trials multiplied, the worst opposition coming from Carmelites who opposed the Reform, for a man's enemies are those of his own household and persecution from one's own is more difficult to bear than persecution from strangers. She was called a gadabout, a "contumacious woman", and some shocking calumnies about her moral character were circulated; friends died, supporters fell away and with each journey her health deteriorated, yet *La Madre* seemed wrapped in serenity and when she wrote on prayer in these last years her theme was the Blessed Trinity.

On a journey from Burgos to Avila in 1582 she was asked to make a detour to Alba de Tormes, town of the grim Duke of Alva; the Duchess, a generous benefactor, had asked for her. The journey took several days; at one hamlet where the nuns stopped for the night, they could not get as much as an egg for Teresa who had fainted several times that day. Finally they came to Alba and its poor little convent. It was the end of the road. Realising that her end was near, Teresa asked for the Last Sacraments; then, as though the Grand Inquisitor were standing there to hear, she declared, "I die a daughter of the Church; I hope to be saved through the merits of Christ." When Holy Communion was brought she exclaimed, "Lord, it is time to set out; may this journey be a good one." Again and again she murmured the verse from Psalm 50, "A humble and contrite heart, O Lord, thou wilt not despise." It was October 4, the feast of St Francis of Assisi, the very day in 1582 when Pope Gregory XIII changed the calendar, adding the famous eleven days, so by the new reckoning it was 15 October. But for Teresa of Jesus time was no more; life, the brief night in a wretched inn, was over. God was her all *forever. . . and forever. . . and forever.*

Teresa and prayer

In 1970 Pope Paul included St Teresa of Avila and St Catherine of Siena among the Doctors of the Church. A Doctor of the Church is a canonised saint who is an expert, a specialist – if one can use such terms – in the knowledge of God and the sacred, in knowledge of the spiritual life, a knowledge derived from revealed truth; far from keeping this knowledge to themselves, these saints teach, explain and share it for the good of the people of God and indeed for the benefit of all mankind. St Teresa and St Catherine were the first of their sex to receive this title and it is noteworthy that neither had received much education or any theological training.

It will be remembered that Teresa was apprenticed to spiritual reading by her Uncle Pedro. In fact she was thrown in at the deep end, St Jerome and St Gregory the Great not being the easiest spiritual writers to cope with. Their many scriptural quotations and their comments on Gospel incidents led her to slow, reflective reading of both Old and New Testaments.

She also read a four-volume *Life of Christ*, written by Ludolph of Saxony, a Carthusian of the fourteenth century; this was immensely popular throughout Europe; it was one of the two books responsible for the conversion of Ignatius Loyola; a century after Teresa's time we find St Francis de Sales recommending it to Madame de Chantal, Foundress of the Visitation nuns and later a canonised saint. It provided easy access to the gospels, dwelling on the mysteries of Christ;[1] it explained what prayer was and

devoted long passages to such themes for prayerful consideration as the Infancy, the Public Life and Passion of Christ,
especially the Seven Words from the Cross, and was evidently the fruit of Ludolph's own meditations in the peace and
solitude of a Carthusian cell. This work also impelled her to
read the scriptures. The great English translator of her
works, Professor Allison Peers, states that so steeped was
she in biblical phraseology that it is difficult to know when
she is consciously quoting and when she is not.

    When asking advice about her experiences in prayer she
usually enquired if these things were in conformity with
Scripture and with the teaching of the Church. In a passage
on prayer, she writes:

> I have always been very fond of the words of the
> gospels, especially the words of our Lord himself,
> just as he spoke them; I have found more recol-
> lection in them than in the most carefully planned
> books.

The abiding truth that dominated her, one might say, from
the cradle to the grave is summed up in the well-known
lines found written on a bookmark she kept in her Office-
book:

> Let nothing disturb you —
> Be not afraid —
> All things pass —
> God never changes.
> Patience obtains all.
> To have God
> Is to lack nothing
> For God is all-sufficing.

"*Todo es nada*. All—the world, life, self—is nothing. God is
all." This basic thought led her to detach herself from what
offends God, from all that was not likely to lead her to
God, and above all from self. Her preoccupation with God
might suggest that fraternal charity was neglected, but in
fact, even in her early years in the Incarnation, she excelled

in thought for others. She undertook the care of a nun
suffering from a slow and dreadful disease and nursed her
until she died; this disagreeable task must have been especially repugnant to Teresa, by nature delicate and extremely
fastidious.

Later, in the convents of the Reform, she took upon herself the lion's share of the work, in the kitchen, at her spinning wheel. "Never a moment idle," declared a nun who
knew her well. In her letters to the many new foundations
we see her care for all the sisters. She like to stress that love
of the neighbour was one of the touchstones of true
sanctity:

> Progress in prayer has nothing to do with enjoying
> many and great consolations, or with raptures,
> visions or other favours of that sort, given by God,
> the value of which we cannot know in this life. . .
> No, sisters, true humility, thinking oneself the worst
> of all, acting for the profit and good of the neigh-
> bour, obedience and mortification—these are the
> true spiritual currency, the coin that ensures us an
> unfailing income, a perpetual inheritance. . . But I
> have noticed in certain persons, and on account of
> our sins they are not many, that the more they give
> themselves to prayer, the more attentive they are to
> the needs of their neighbour. I do not believe we
> can ever attain perfect love for our neighbour unless
> it has its roots in the love of God.

She continually emphasised that it is possible to become
closely united to God, to advance far in prayer, without
experiencing visions and other favours. Many saints who
were great contemplatives never had a vision; St Vincent de
Paul, for instance, whose immense apostolate of charity—
or, rather, justice and charity, for he held that if there were
justice for all there would be little need of material charity—
his love of the neighbour stemmed from his spirit of prayer,
yet he never had a vision or revelation. And St Boniface
shrewdly remarks that if everyone who saw a vision was a

saint, Balaam and his ass qualified for canonisation!

I am not competent to discuss her visions, locutions and other phenomena, or the heights she reached in prayer and union with God. These can be read in the various lives of the saint or, at first hand, in her own *Autobiography*, written at the command of her confessor. Readers led by similar ways will, like Teresa, have the good sense to find themselves a good director, and to obey him absolutely. Remember Maddalena de la Cruz! The devil can act the angel to deceive us.

Speaking of directors, Teresa like them to be (1) learned; (2) holy and (3) prudent. If possible she like a combination of (1) and (2) and if we wonder at her giving learning priority it must be remembered that those were the times before the Council of Trent when seminaries, as we know them, were non-existent and when many priests were ordained on the strength of a certificate of character from a prelate who might never have seen or heard of a candidate until he presented himself for such a certificate. While Sr Teresa liked prudent directors, she had little use for the over-prudent and timid who could prove more of a hindrance than help. She describes the plight of some Carmelites who had that kind of director: "Poor souls! He would only let them advance (in prayer) at snail's pace. They might have been soaring like eagles, but he kept them like hens with their feet tied."

Instead of following Teresa to the great spiritual heights she herself attained, it may be more helpful for us to consider her teaching on prayer—private, personal prayer—under the headings our Lord gave for that in the Sermon on the Mount. He was speaking to ordinary people like us and the points he made were: (1) to seek solitude; (2) to avoid gabbling, to mean what we say; (3) he gave us the *Our Father*, the perfect prayer. I asked a Scripture scholar why our Lord told us to go "into our own rooms", when he himself had not that luxury; he found privacy in the desert, on a hillside, in a garden. I was told that the word Christ used, *tameoin*, was originally a term meaning the room where a steward stored goods but that later it came to mean any secluded place, where one could be sure of being alone.

The subsequent lines in St Matthew explain why solitude is necessary; it helps us to avoid hypocrisy; for there is a bit of a hypocrite in each of us, we tend to adopt a pose in public. When alone one is more oneself, more sincere, therefore more humble. And when we stand humbly before God with all our defences down, he is drawn to us and prayer becomes for us as it did for Teresa, when she gave up worrying about what others thought of her, a kind of spiritual therapy and healing.

Before quoting her on solitude as the best climate for prayer, there are two men of this country and century who have experienced this, who might be mentioned. Matt Talbot, waiting for loads of timber to arrive at Martin's yard, would go between the stacks of planks out of sight of his fellow-workers, and pray until the next load came. The other men knew this, and respected his need to be alone with God; if they had to go in his direction, they shouted to one another or whistled or sang to give him time to rise from his knees before they approached him. Fr Aidan McGrath, enduring an enforced solitary confinement in a Chinese prison, tells us that it was the best opportunity for prayer he ever had.

When St Teresa founded the first convent of the Reform she saw to it that each nun had a cell to herself and there were huts or hermitages in the garden where a Sister might be alone if she wished to pray outdoors. Referring to solitude, Teresa says:

> It is easy to keep silence if one is alone. Getting used to solitude is a great help to prayer for it is impossible to speak to God and the world at the same time. When we resolve to devote to God this brief period of our day, let us give it to him freely

and with our minds unoccupied with other things. For our time is lent to us. Those who are able to shut themselves up in this inner room, this little heaven of the soul, and who avoid distractions may be sure that they are on the right road. They will journey a long way in a short time like a ship with a fair and following wind.

She tells us that when she herself started to pray she sought solitude; she found it helpful to think of Christ at times when *he* was alone, particularly during the Passion and at that unknown hour on Easter morning when he rose from the dead. She reminds us that when we withdraw from the company of others to pray, we do so to come into the presence of God. Like all the spiritual writers on prayer, she stresses the need of pausing to recollect ourselves before prayer, to realise in whose presence we are, to think of what he is and what we are. She found St Augustine a help —his saying that he sought God everywhere and finally found him within his own soul.

When praying alone outdoors the works of God's hand, the skies, the stars, water, snow, growing things, helped her to think of and praise the Creator of all. She insists on sincerity. "God likes us to speak frankly; we should not be bashful with him." But she returns again and again to the need of withdrawal from all that might distract from the conversation, the dialogue with God, and deplores the fact that many live so much on the surface that they never give themselves a chance of really praying.

As regards Christ's remarks about not using too many words, as the heathens do, Teresa echoes his advice:

> We should not be satisfied with words alone. When I say the *Creed* it seems to me right and indeed obligatory that I should understand and know what it is I believe, and when I say the *Our Father* my love should make me want to understand who this Father of ours is and who the Master who taught us

this prayer. . . The Lord does not want us to break
our heads chattering at him; he values more the
words that spring from the heart than any ready-
made prayer. . .

One reason why more are not granted the grace of
contemplation is because people shut their ears to
his voice. For they like the sound of their own
voices and repeat many vocal prayers in a great
hurry, as though they were anxious to finish their
task of saying them daily. So, when the Lord comes
to put, as I may say, his kingdom in their hands,
they do not accept it, but think that they are doing
better by continuing to recite their prayers, which
prayers are really only distracting them from the
real purpose of prayer. . . For prayer is nothing
more than friendly, familiar conversation with God
who we know loves us.

For those to whom the Lord says "Go up higher, friend",
she illumines every step of the way, but she warns that the
way of higher contemplation is hard, "a path going uphill
all the way, right to the very end." She is careful to state
how far a soul can advance by its own efforts and how
dangerous it is to try to elevate oneself beyond this before,
and unless, the Lord calls. The best one can do is to dispose
oneself. To presume that one can go higher oneself, she
says, is to fall back into aridity, for it shows a want of
humility, that foundation-stone of prayer and the entire
spiritual life.

She adds further warnings against complacency and self-
persuasion, watching ourselves to see how we are praying or
what stage we have reached; this leads to hypocrisy; and she
cites the case of a few persons she knew who imagined
themselves to be saints: "They frightened me more," says
Teresa, "than all the sinners I ever met."

When she treats of the Lord's own prayer, the *Our
Father*, she is magnificent. So much so that you must read
her for yourselves. You will find it in one of her books, *The*

Way of Perfection, chapters 27 to 42. Incidentally, in the chapters on the phrase "Give us this day our daily bread", she is very helpful on preparation for and thanksgiving after Holy Communion. Here, I will content myself with quoting her words on the excellence of the *Paternoster*, a rich legacy left by our Lord to each one of us:

> The sublimity of this prayer from the gospels is something for which we should greatly praise the Lord. . . So well did he compose it that each may use it in his or her own way. I am astonished when I consider that in its few words are enshrined all contemplation and all perfection. If we study it no other book seems necessary; in it our Lord teaches us how to pray—the whole method from the beginnings of mental prayer of the Prayer of Quiet and Union. . .
>
> It would be a good thing for us to consider that he has taught this prayer to each one of us individually, and that he is continually teaching it to us. . . I have often wondered why he did not expound this prayer in greater detail. Then it occurred to me that, since he meant it as a general prayer for the use of all, everyone could interpret it as he thought right, ask for what he wants and find comfort in doing so. . . Very few who say the *Our Father* well are deceived by the devil.

And she goes on to tell of a very old nun who came to her one day in great distress saying that she did not know how to practise mental prayer. When Teresa questioned her she found that this nun spent almost three hours daily saying the *Paternoster* two or three times and had been raised to pure contemplation and union with God. Moreover, her life as a religious, her practice of virtue and her love of the neighbour was very perfect.

Those who are familiar with St Teresa's writings will know how in one book, her *Autobiography*, she compares the stages of prayer to the watering of a garden. The first

stage, or rather way, and the most laborious, drawing water
from a well with a bucket; the second by a mechanical con-
traption used in the Spain of her time; the third by irriga-
tion, and the fourth and far most effective—but beyond the
power of the gardener to bring about—the blessed rain from
heaven, so welcome on the parched lands of Castile. Teresa
loved to think about water, its qualities, its uses; it reminded
her of the Water of Life for which the Samaritan woman
asked Christ. The sight of a river or lake or fountain was
enough to send her thoughts back to the giver of the Living
Water.

In another work, *The Interior Castle*, she sees the soul as
a huge diamond, a diamond castle or mansion with several
rooms—in one place she says seven rooms, in another she
says countless rooms, the central one the dwelling-place
of the Blessed Trinity, the Triune God. To pray is to enter
this vast castle of the soul and move stage by stage towards
that inner room.

One does not need to be highly intelligent or well
educated to make that journey. One man who followed her
that far was our poor man of Dublin, Matt Talbot; illiterate
for his first thirty years he slowly, laboriously taught himself to read; he read her works and was led by the Spirit on
the same high way as Teresa. However, for our comfort, the
saint stresses that God does not lead souls by the same
road; "there are as many different ways to him as there are
souls," so she leaves us free to take the path best suited to
ourselves and does not advocate any particular method.

It may be asked what her influence was in her own time
and country and what relevance, if any, she has for modern
times. She had a natural gift for influencing and attracting
people. As a girl she ruled her brothers. Even when she herself abandoned prayer for a time in that period she later
called "my wasted years", she induced her father to practise
mental prayer and lent him helpful books. In the convents
of the Reform sanctity became the norm, the nuns seeming

to catch the spirit, the holiness, the love of God that inflamed *La Madre*. Their example and that of the discalced, barefoot friars, living so poorly, so austerely in their little convents, exerted great influence in Spain at a time when that nation needed precisely that example.

God seems to raise up saints at certain times and in certain countries to meet needs of that time and place. Teresa, Ignatius and John of the Cross are but three of eighteen canonised saints of sixteenth-century Spain—and there were as many blessed for the same century and kingdom. By the middle of that century the Spanish people seemed to have realised all possible dreams. Their fathers' generation had finally driven out the Moors who for almost eight centuries had occupied the country. Spaniards had marched on and conquered Mexico, colonised Florida, traversed the Mississippi plains; they were the first to sight the Pacific, to scale the Andes, to sail around the world.

The nation had become dizzy from sheer achievement, but now there were no more territories to discover, no more peoples to conquer. While the religious debates and the religious wars devastated Europe the great wall of the Pyrenees had formed a protective barrier for Spain; within her boundaries the Inquisition had crushed, cruelly but effectually (and it must be remembered, not any more cruelly than what was being done elsewhere in the name of religion), any deviations from orthodoxy that appeared. The wealth of the New World had been unloaded on the quays of Cadiz and Seville; and yet, a general sense of disenchantment prevailed.

It was then that Teresa became known, Teresa with her watchword, "All things pass, and we with them. God alone remains. All is nothing. God is all." To a people satiated with success and power and wealth, a people heading towards decadence, she was a sign of the imperishable, the only lasting good. She bore witness to the reality of the living God, to the fact that prayer is an encounter with

God. The doctrine of grace and justification being debated
so seriously by the reforming Council of Trent was *lived* by
Teresa, for God gave her not only the charismatic gift of
experiencing such realities, but also of expressing them
simply in writings that are the inheritance of Christians and
of many non-Christians of her time and since.

Her teaching has relevance for our century also. You
recall Edith Stein, a Jewish professor of philosophy in
Germany, a professed atheist; she came on a copy of
Teresa's *Autobiography* seemingly by chance, stayed up all
night to read it and said, "That's the truth"; she became a
Catholic, a Carmelite, a very holy one, and died in one of
Hitler's concentration camps. And there is the Chinese, Dr
John Wu, who passed from Buddhism to Protestantism,
thence to Catholicism and whose book on Teresian prayer,
The Interior Carmel, has long been a classic.

More recently a young Japanese, a Shintoist, was converted through Teresa's writings, though he had to learn
French to read them. The Taizé Community has close links
with the present community in St Joseph's, Avila; and most
surprising of all, at the Marxist Congress in Salzburg in
1965 Garaudy, a leading French Communist, declared,
"For us Marxists St Teresa and St John of the Cross are
high examples of human love."

For our time, too, she is a sign, a witness to the reality
of God. We notice the pollution of the atmosphere, the
earth, the oceans, but we perhaps fail to notice the more
insidious pollution caused by a universal atheism, a lack of
faith in God. Modern man needs, though he may not be
aware of his need, affirmation, assurance of the real, the
true, the lasting, the only good. Teresa confronts him,
speaking with the authority of a lived experience: "There is
a God. I have met him in prayer, listened to him when he
spoke to me."

Fr Clemens Tillman, the Munich catechist, speaking to
preachers and teachers, said: "*When you speak of God and*

the sacred, speak reverently; when you speak of virtue and the moral law, speak persuasively; when you speak of the truths of faith, speak with authority and conviction." That is how Teresa of Jesus spoke to the people of her time and country. That is how she still speaks to the world.

Mary Purcell

5 St Vincent de Paul

His life, times and spirituality

On the evening of Good Friday 1974 the BBC television authorities selected for showing on Channel 2 a French film that had been made more than twenty-five years before. The film was *Monsieur Vincent*. It had had a very favourable reception in France when it first appeared, as indeed it did also in Britain. When it was first shown in the old Savoy cinema here in Dublin, it had a very short run; much shorter than it had in London's West End cinemas. Why it failed to appeal to the Irish public, one cannot say. Was it that there was a dimension missing to the film (as indeed there was) which made it unsatisfying to an Irish audience in a way that was overlooked by audiences in other countries?

Even after twenty-five years or more which have seen so much change in film technique, *Monsieur Vincent*, with Pierre Fresnay playing the part of the saint, has worn well. Had it not done so, BBC 2 would not have gone back so far in years to find a film suitable for showing on Good Friday afternoon.

The film has much human interest in it, yet it fails to capture the whole man that was Vincent de Paul. Not indeed that any medium will catch him easily, for as Daniel Rops remarked about him: "His works surround him like a forest and his humility envelops him like a fog." In the film it is not the forest nor the fog that conceals the saint. It is

the fact that the producer and the script writer have overlooked and forgotten Good Friday. And Good Friday—and
above all the man on the centre cross—was everything to M.
Vincent. The forest of good works had not yet grown up
around him nor the fog of his humility become quite so
dense when, in 1631, he wrote: "Let us remember that we
live in Jesus Christ through the death of Jesus Christ, that
we should die in Jesus Christ through the life of Jesus
Christ; that our life should be hidden in Jesus Christ; and
that to die like Jesus Christ, we must live like Jesus Christ."
Little doubt there about the starting and finishing point of
all activity.

Superimposed on the opening shot of French countryside in the film is the year 1617. The year was well chosen.
It was not the year that Vincent de Paul was born. M.
Vincent was then thirty-six years of age. The opening scene
of the film depicts this thirty-six-year-old priest descending
from a stage coach on a July day and walking with a knap-
sack over his back into a small village of which he had
recently been appointed parish priest. As a Christian parish
it was decadent, almost dead. The parish church housed
animals, and the people were indifferent, if not positively
hostile, to the coming of the new parish priest. With the
love of God in his heart, with the strength of his arm and
the sweat of his brow, M. Vincent started to restore the
church.

In later years he would be fond of saying: "Let us love
God, yes, let us love God, but let it be with the strength of
our arm and the sweat of our brow"; and Chatillon-les-
Dombes—for that was the name of the parish—saw the
strength of M. Vincent's arm and the sweat of his brow.
He was only about three weeks in the parish when, as he
was vesting for Mass on an August Sunday, word was
brought to him that there was a family so badly in want in
the parish that, if food was not brought to them quickly,
they would be in danger of death. M. Vincent appealed on

their behalf. He preached a charity sermon that was so effective that the family were overwhelmed with food and drink and clothing that afternoon. It would seem that after the seven years of famine, the seven years of plenty were to be telescoped into one day.

M. Vincent saw that generosity needed not only to be tapped, but to be piped and stored and refined. And so very shortly after that experience he set up the Confraternity of Charity, a group of caring women in the parish who would see that not only would the meals be provided for Sundays but for weekdays as well; that the meals, so to speak, would not only be cooked, but be put on wheels. . .

There is drama in that opening part of the film *Monsieur Vincent*. Historically speaking, there was already quite an amount of drama in the life of the thirty-six-year-old priest. His coming to Chatillon-les-Dombes was something of an escape. For some four years he had been living in one of France's stately homes. The de Gondi family were landed gentry, and M. Vincent de Paul had been employed by them to act as tutor to their three children, the youngest of whom had only recently been born. The tutor lived in: his board and lodging probably made up most of his salary. The lady of the house was a good woman: she was also scrupulous. Besides being tutor to her sons, she found him to be a good confessor and adviser.

Then quite suddenly—and almost without any intimations of what he was going to do, but with the consent of his director Cardinal de Berulle—M. Vincent left the stately home. Was it that he felt life too constricting in this household, or was the Spirit of God already breathing on him and inviting him to take the wide world as his parish? We do not know. We do know, however, that his sudden departure left a void in the house. Madame de Gondi relapsed into scrupulosity again, and a manhunt was started for M. Vincent. She went out herself, and in the winter of 1617 finally tracked him down in Chatillon-les-Dombes.

She succeeded in persuading M. Vincent to return, but only after he had consulted with Cardinal de Berulle.

The year 1617 had been a dramatic year for M. Vincent. It was now December. The previous January, he had been out and about on the de Gondi estates and he had heard the confession of a dying man. Later that day in January 1617, Madame de Gondi called on the dying man. He told her that had not M. Vincent called that morning, he would have lost his soul. He had been making bad confessions for years, but the grace of God had shone out that morning, and through M. Vincent he had been sincerely and lastingly reconciled to God.

That January month in 1617 had been a busy month for M. Vincent because with the encouragement of Madame de Gondi, M. Vincent went around the estate preaching on the sacrament of penance and particularly on the advantages to be derived from general confessions. His preaching was so successful that clergy from the neighbouring parishes and districts had to be called in to cope with the number of penitents.

So the year 1617—from January to December—had been a full one for M. Vincent. And although the producer of the film *Monsieur Vincent* may not have known it when he superimposed the year 1617 on that opening scene of the French countryside, he was pointing up what was spiritually the most significant year in the life of St Vincent de Paul. For from St Vincent's experience of the dying man's confession and the success of his preaching on the de Gondi estates, was to be born his work of preaching missions, focused on the theme of reconciliation. From that was to be born in turn the need to have good seminaries to train those preparing for the priesthood and thus secure that they would be well educated to carry on the work of reconciling men with God. From that in turn was to be born the work of keeping priests up-to-date in their knowledge of theology and in the living of good lives. So first in Paris,

and then elsewhere, St Vincent organised the Tuesday Conferences, which in their own way were the forerunners of
our renewal courses today.

From his experience at Chatillon-les-Dombes were to be
born the Ladies of Charity, and from them the Daughters
of Charity. The monies which St Vincent and St Louise de
Marillac managed to persuade the Ladies of Charity to give
and to collect were to be channelled through the Daughters
of Charity so that they not only reached the right homes
and the deserving poor, but came enveloped in the charity
of Christ. From all this was to be born that elaborate organ-
isation of relief work which he managed to set up in the
midst of the civil war then ravaging France, and the caring
for the thousands of sick to whom our modern hospitals
and clinics would have been just a delirious dream.

1617 was a significant—and I think perhaps the most
significant—year for the development of all those works
which M. Vincent fathered, and which still cluster around
his name, and claim him as architect, builder or founder.

But there had been drama, and perhaps deeper drama, in
the person and soul of St Vincent prior to 1617. In the
devil's dictionary a saint is described as a "dead sinner
revised and edited". It is a somewhat cynical definition, as
if the canonical process of canonisation was a sort of dry-
cleaning, removing all stains and blemishes from the fabric
of their temperaments and behaviour. There is only one
human character whom the Church claims to have been
without blemish, and that from the moment of her conception. All the saints of the Church but our Lady are sinners,
revised and edited. . . But the revision and the editing have
been done by themselves in their lifetime. Rather should I
say that it has been done by themselves for the glory of
God the Father through the grace of our Lord Jesus Christ
and by the working of the Holy Spirit. Vincent de Paul is a
sinner revised and edited. Revision and editing there was
need of, and such revision and editing cannot be done with-

out cutting and the red pencil of suffering such as described
by Hopkins:

O the mind, mind has mountains; cliffs of fall
Frightful, sheer, no-man-fathomed.

As a priest of thirty years of age who may have been
slipping into the living grave of mediocrity, he met in the
university society of Paris a priest-professor in the Sor-
bonne. This priest had confided in M. Vincent that he was
undergoing a crisis of identity not as a priest, but as a
Christian. He felt that he was losing the faith. St Vincent
counselled him, and then with one of those mysterious
gestures of generosity which were probably characteristic of
his nature, he undertook to assume the temptations the
professor was suffering.

For three or four years M. Vincent underwent an experience such as Cardinal Newman describes: "The night is dark
and I am far from home." The first streaks of dawn streamed
across the horizons of his mind when he decided to give
himself to Christ in the poor. It was then that the crisis of
faith was surmounted. The conviction was burned into him
—and it was never to leave him—that "faith apart from
works is barren"; that "faith is completed by works". With
these two convictions which he now shared with St James
he became in a new way, and was called, "the friend of
God."

Revision and editing can be done by God's mysterious
red pencil of mental suffering. There are other gentle
agencies, and among these was one whom St Vincent used
to refer to as the "gentle bishop of Geneva", whom we
know today as St Francis de Sales. They met in Paris almost
immediately after the eventful year of 1617. There they
came to know each other. How one exchanges the fruits of
the Spirit—joy, peace, courtesy, kindness—with another will
never be fully revealed to us, but that such an exchange
took place between Francis de Sales and St Vincent there is

little doubt. That an exchange did take place is certain, for after nine months, when the bishop had to return to his diocese in the south-east of France, he asked M. Vincent to take over the direction of the superior of the Visitation nuns in Paris whom we now know as St Jane Frances de Chantal. For his part M. Vincent, many years later, whenever he wanted to conjure up in his mind an idea of the patience and goodness of God, would think of the reflection of it that he had seen in Francis de Sales, the gentle bishop of Geneva.

It has been said that had not St Vincent met St Francis de Sales during that year 1618, he might have remained a rather pessimistic, melancholic character. It would seem certain that he learned from St Francis to be less inhibited in unfolding the desires of his heart in prayer—which is one of St Thomas Aquinas' definitions of prayer.

The work of revising and editing that would make Vincent de Paul the saint he was to become did not end with his meetings with the priest-professor in Paris and with St Francis de Sales. He would realise with St Paul that "we are God's workmanship", and that his grace and his love would play on him as the spring sunshine does on the earth until the harvest is ripe for the reaping. He was to realise, too, that God's workmanship would be done on him not in a closed workshop, but as he moved out in search of the poor and the neglected. The neglected, I think, meant for him what the Latin word *neglecti* means—the "unchosen". He would see God's workmanship being done—the work of revising and editing—in himself as he gave himself to God in the person of the neighbour. Indeed, one of his most often repeated phrases is "Let us give ourselves to God."

Yes, let us give ourselves to God, and when that is being done, then with security and with the energy of God—with the "agape" of God—one can give oneself to the neighbour, and find God there. The work of revising and editing would go on not only in the quietness of prayer on the mountain of transfiguration, but in the plain places amongst the deaf, the sick, the paralysed. His often quoted counsel to the Daughters of Charity was that they were to have "no monastery but the sick room, no cell but the hired lodging, no chapel but the parish church, no cloister but the street."

Today, of course, there are numerous orders of uncloistered sisters. But it is worth noting that the first person ever to take women out of the cloister and allow them to bring the religious life into the streets and market-place was Vincent de Paul.

We left M. Vincent with St Francis de Sales, and that was in 1618. He was to live for another forty-two years. The daughters of Charity lived uncloistered lives and Vincent's life was also an uncloistered one. He was to be called to assist King Louis XIII as he lay dying. He was to become an adviser to the Queen who was to succeed Louis as Regent until her son became of age to reign. It was she who appointed M. Vincent to what was known then as the "Council of Conscience" in France: it was, one might say, the government department which saw to it—or rather was intended to see to it—that only worthy candidates were appointed to be bishops. This brought him into conflict with the man who was prime minister of the day, Cardinal Mazarin.

M. Vincent de Paul could not be bought, and at least on two occasions at a time of national crisis, M. Vincent told this very powerful political figure that he was accountable to his God for his actions. In a very real sense he was the Keeper of the Queen's conscience. . . Cardinal Mazarin, after nine years, quietly managed to drop him from the Council and felt more at ease when he was rid of this fearless priest. His movement in and out of the royal palace did not so absorb him that he had not time to be—almost without his being aware of it—the parish priest of the distressed areas of the then known world.

Ireland was suffering under the ravaging campaigns of

Cromwell. M. Vincent knew it, and managed to send six of his priests, most of them Irishmen, to Ireland to conduct missions and to give the sacraments to the hunted Catholic population. He had a few priests in England and further north in Scotland. Down on the shores of Africa, he organised and managed what today would be regarded as a Red Cross operation—tracing Frenchmen who had been taken prisoners by the Turks and paying out large sums of money to have them released. Through the court in Warsaw, he established a house for priests to carry on the work of preaching.

I have picked only a few of the trees of that forest of works which surround him, and which makes it a little difficult to focus in our mind's eye this rounded and sainted character. A favourite word of his was "conference". He was constantly calling conferences—of his priests, of his Daughters of Charity, of men to be ordained, conferences of priests already ordained, conferences of those rich Ladies of Charity whom he had persuaded, and made it fashionable, to yield up their necklaces and jewels for the alleviation of distress. The conferences that M. Vincent would call were not just talking shops. Like everything else, they were called for action.

Could you imagine in these days of conferences a small conference made up of the following personalities known to us all. Mother Teresa of Calcutta; beside her is seated Martin Luther King because of his interest in the problems of race discrimination. On the other hand of Mother Teresa is Frank Duff, because of his sustained and long interest in the lay apostolate. Next to him is Dr Kissinger, present because of his skill and patience in diplomacy. Next to him is Pope Paul VI, present because of his dedication to the Church and his combination of compassion of heart and uncompromising stand for Christian principles. Pope Paul evokes the memory of his predecessor—and his radiant geniality. Now if you can imagine that conference being

dissolved in heaven into one person, you will have caught
something of the genius, the goodness and the breadth of
concern of St Vincent de Paul.

I mention all these names in order to make some assess-
ment of that forest of works which he originated and the
spirit in which he had set about the planning of the forest.
He would vehemently object to my use of the word "origin-
ate". He was very insistent on the fact that he had originated
nothing: that all the initiative had lain always with God. He
had a very great fear of anticipating Divine Providence. The
fog of humility came down thicker and thicker on him. His
protestations about his own unworthiness and sinfulness
can be disconcerting, exaggerated and almost bordering on
the insincere. But then the sharpness and intensity of the
vision he had been given of Christ suffering in the poor, the
sick and the unchosen may have in its brightness so dazzled
him that he could see "only Jesus", and had lost sight of
himself, or could only see the darkness that cast a shadow
on the work.

At the close of the film *Monsieur Vincent* there is a
piece of dialogue between the saint and Queen Anne of
Austria. If it is imaginary, it is very much in the character
of the saint. In his eightieth year, his head now sunk into
his shoulders, the dark eyes reflecting the depths within the
man, the mouth and lips faintly suggesting the Gascon wit
that was his, he is being congratulated by the Queen on the
achievements of his life. Reflecting and looking into the
middle distance, he mutters "I have done nothing." "But
M. Vincent, look at the foundlings you have saved, the sick
and poor you have provided for, your work for the Church
in France and other countries. . ." In the same low tone of
voice, M. Vincent says again, "I have done nothing.
Nothing." The Queen becomes a little impatient: "Well, if
you have done nothing, what about us, how can we face
our Judge, what have we got to do?" There is a pause. And
then M. Vincent lifts his head, looks into the Queen's face
and slowly speaks one word: "*Davantage*." "More."

Vincent de Paul and prayer

If the works of St Vincent surround him like a forest, and his humility envelops him like a fog, he himself chose to remain silent about what he was experiencing in the midst of the forest and in the density of the fog. About the depth of his own inner life of prayer he was rather uncommunicative. He spoke about no visions that were ever given to him—except one. After the death of St Jane Frances de Chantal—as he prayed for her at the memento of the dead at Mass—he seemed to see three globes: one merged into another and then that globe merged into a larger one and he was given to understand that the soul of St Jane Frances was united with that of St Francis de Sales, and that both were hidden now in the depths of the mystery of the Trinity.

Remaining rather silent about his own inner life of prayer did not prevent him from sharing with people some of his convictions about prayer and its place in the lives of those with whom he talked or corresponded. One of his most celebrated utterances was "Give me a man of prayer and he will be capable of everything."

He published no book on prayer, but in his letters and conferences there are scattered maxims, hints, counsels on prayer. Every letter he wrote (and he wrote about 40,000 of which only some 3,000 are today extant) began with a prayer—very similar to that greeting which begins the greatest of our prayers, the Mass: "May the Grace of our Lord Jesus Christ be with us for ever." He gave conferences to his community of priests and brothers and to the Daughters of Charity. But taking notes during them displeased him. So his ideas on prayer were either surreptitiously taken down as he spoke, or jotted down from memory afterwards.

In his mature years he advised each of his priests to spend one hour in mental prayer every day, convinced as he was of its importance as the beginning of any day's work that was to be done for and with Jesus Christ. He remarked in one of his conferences that "the grace of vocation is attached to prayer and the grace of prayer to the grace of rising." So deeply Christ-sprung was all his motivation that the hour's prayer is put forward as a concession to human weakness, for in putting forward the ideal of an hour's prayer in the day he remarks:

> Though we cannot to the full extent imitate Christ our Lord who besides his daily meditation spent whole nights in the prayer of God, we will, however, do it to the best of our poor ability. Therefore all and everyone shall diligently give themselves to mental prayer for one hour every day. . .

He evolved no special method of mental prayer that bears his name today. However, in his counsels about prayer, one can trace the influence of those writers and saints who had speculated more deeply about the nature of prayer. To Cardinal de Berulle of Paris—who was his spiritual director for two years—one can trace the very strong emphasis on the humanity of Christ—Jesus Christ was to be thought and reflected upon in all his states and experiences. To his friend St Francis de Sales can be traced the prominent place that should be given to what the older writers called "affections" in prayer and which we in modern parlance might refer to as the spontaneous unfoldings of the desires of a person's heart after he or she has reflected on some incident in the life of Christ or some passage of Scripture.

The system or method which St Francis de Sales proposes in his classic work, *The Introduction to the Devout*

Life, with its considerations, affections and resolutions was adopted by St Vincent. However, he was an independent-minded man, and one can notice in his counsels and advice the rather strong emphasis he gives to the place of resolutions in prayer. He went so far as to say that mental prayer was useless if it did not end with some resolution that had bearing on life as it was to be lived outside the chapel or oratory. He was not one of those—nor did he want those he directed to become—so heavenly-minded as to be of no earthly use. His method would be that of St James who warns against looking at one's natural face in a mirror and then forgetting what one was like. "Carthusians at home, apostles abroad" was his motto.

Prayer was to issue forth in action and work. The experience of work and action should bring one back to prayer. So the rhythmic cycle would go on: the pendulum-like swing that one notices in the life of Christ—particularly in the gospel of St Luke—between the Christ withdrawn on the mountain in communion with his Father, and the Christ among the people, healing all manner of diseases, preaching "good news to the poor".

Because St Vincent was largely uncommunicative about his own personal prayer—except when it would burst into aspirations at the end of a conference—and because he wrote no work or book on prayer, we can only guess at what were some of those attitudes that were his when, in the silence of prayer, he presented himself—and the suffering world that he had come to know—to God.

The most striking feature of his spirituality is his faith in divine providence. Again and again he comes back to it, and to the allied concept of prudence. "We must abandon ourselves to God's providence and take great care not to run ahead of it. The works of God achieve themselves, and those that are not his soon perish. Rest assured of that saying, which may seem a paradox, that he who hurries delays the things of God... The good God always takes care of our affairs when we see to his. What happiness to be in the place God has put us, and what unhappiness to set ourselves up where he was not called us!"

Trusting in providence, he was untroubled by the small number of those who offered to join his community, preferring thus "to honour the small number of disciples who were given to the Son of God", and bore with astonishing equanimity the loss of some of his best men through disease and plague, particularly in Madagascar. His waiting for providence gave an impression of tardiness, and often provoked the impatience of his priests. But as he saw it, the forest had grown up without his planting a sapling, or if he did plant the sapling, it was only after he had received some clear unmistakable sign about the soil where it was to be sown.

It is hardly claiming too much for St Vincent to affirm that he patented in his lifetime what we know today as "shared prayer". He would gather around him the Daughters of Charity; they would pray together in silence. Then the saint would ask each sister in turn to tell the group what she had experienced in prayer—all the time eliciting from the saint comment of praise or guidance—while he himself often burst into expressions of spontaneous prayer. The Daughers of Charity were encouraged in this practice (known as "repetitions of prayer"), "to empty themselves of themselves [a favourite phrase of the saint] and allow God to act."

Here is a short passage from the saint which is relevant for anyone who wants to climb the mountain of the Lord in prayer:

When the repetitions of prayer are held I inwardly reflect how comes it that some make so little progress in this holy exercise of meditation; there is reason to fear that the cause of this evil is that they do not mortify themselves enough and that they allow too much freedom to their senses. Read what the most skilled masters in the spiritual life have written on this question of prayer, and you will see that they unanimously hold that the practice of mortification is absolutely necessary to pray well, and that the proper disposition for prayer is not merely to mortify the eyes, the tongue, the ears and the other exterior senses, but also the faculties of the soul, the understanding, the memory and the will; by this means mortification will dispose us to pray well and reciprocally prayer will help us to mortify ourselves.

Let the final word be with the saint himself. It says much for his confidence in youth that at the age of seventy-five he appointed as superior of one of his houses a young priest who was twenty-seven years of age. Human prudence might have said he was too young. But prudence, like providence, can be daring. The young priest had the good sense to go to the saint for some advice on how to guide his community, and he had the better sense to write down immediately afterwards what the saint, in the evening of his life, had said to him:

> An important matter, to which you must carefully apply yourself, is to have a wealth of communication with our Lord in prayer. That is the reservoir where you will find the instructions necessary in order that you may acquit yourself properly in the office to which you are going. Whenever you find yourself in doubt, have recourse to God, saying: "O Lord, thou who art the Father of lights, teach me what I must do in this turn of events."
> I give you this advice not only for the occasions you will find distressing, but also in order that you may be enlightened by God in what you will have to teach... And I have to tell you that in contributing to the salvation of others one may get lost. Wherefore, in order not to fall into the misfortune of Saul or Judas, it is necessary to attach yourself inseparably

to our Saviour, and, lifting up to him your heart and soul, to say to him often: "O Lord, do not permit me to lose myself miserably as I try to save others; be thou my shepherd, and do not deny me the graces you communicate to others through my intervention and through the functions of my ministry." You ought also to have recourse to prayer in order to ask our Saviour for the things which those in your care have need of. Believe most certainly that you will reap a better harvest in this way than in any other. Jesus Christ, on whom you could model your whole conduct of affairs, was not content with preaching and good works, nor with fasting, nor with shedding his blood and dying for us; for to all this he added prayer. He had no need to pray for himself; it was for us then that he prayed so often, in order that we might learn to do the same, both in what concerns ourselves, and in what concerns those of whom we should be the saviours along with him.

This passage epitomises St Vincent's essential teaching on prayer, which for us today is as relevant as it was in the seventeenth century, and still will be in the twenty-first century and beyond.

Richard McCullen, CM

6   St Alphonsus Liguori

His life, times and spirituality

To meet St Alphonsus, I invite you to pass over with me to
another place, to Naples in the south; and to another time,
to the slower world of horse power, sedan chairs and foot-
men—the 18th century. The life of Alphonsus spans this
century; born not long after the battle of the Boyne, he
died two years before the storming of the Bastille. It was
not the best of times. Religion, in poor shape after the wars
of the previous century, tended to lose heart and hope
under the creeping influence of Jansenism. Optimism had
passed to the philosophers who promoted reason above
faith to be the judge of all reality. To answer the needs of
the time, a man was sent by God, Alphonsus de Liguori. He
dominates the spirituality of the age.

1696:   Born at Naples. At twelve he began the study of law
        at the university, qualifying in canon and civil law at
        sixteen (four years ahead of time).
1726:   Abandoning the law, he was ordained priest.
1731:   Moved to Scala, where he helped found the Redemp-
        toristine nuns, and later established the Redemptor-
        ists.
1749:   Papal approval for the new congregation.
1762:   Ordained bishop of St Agatha dei Goti.
1775:   Resigned due to ill-health, returning to his congre-
        gation.
1787:   Died at Pagani.
1839:   Canonisation.
1871:   Declared Doctor of the Church.
1960:   Declared patron of confessors and moral theologians.

To give oneself entirely to God

What strikes me most about Alphonsus is the quality emphasised in Church documents: he is a "most zealous" doctor. In the liturgy too he was compared to "incense burning in fire". There is an incendiary quality in the man, the ardour and urgency of total commitment. "To belong wholly to God" (*essere tutti a Dio*), "to give oneself wholly to God" (*darsi tutti a Dio*) are phrases that constantly recur in him. Certainly he needed to be single-minded, single-hearted, and single-souled in the many crises of his life.

Take the crisis of his vocation. His father had other ambitions for him than the Church. So he waged a long war, hot and cold, to break Alphonsus' resolution. The final violent scene, lasting three hours of clinging and tears, was agony for the warm-hearted saint. Later at Scala another crisis developed when all but one of the nine original Redemptorists deserted him. A difficult task at any time, to found a new religious order was doubly so in the kingdom of Naples, where the law banned all religious foundations. Yet Alphonsus doggedly persevered in doing God's work, setting up new communities in spite of repeated failures to win royal approval. This came eventually only after his death.

At the age of sixty-six, in spite of his appeal to the Pope to spare "this old bag of bones", he was made bishop, and became an all-out bishop. He put the diocese in a state of prolonged mission, concentrating his renewal efforts especially on the clergy and seminarians, but neglecting not a single person or church building. When he resigned, he was already half blind and deaf, and so crippled with arthritis that he could scarcely move. Yet, back among his brethren, he prayed and worked as hard as ever; books and letters continued to come until he could write no more.

More than ever in the last years of his life, his utter commitment to God stood him in good stead. He suffered agony of body, and of mind too, with doubts and scruples. On top of this came a final blow. An attempt to get the Rule approved was mismanaged by his representative at Naples, Fr Mazzini, who let the officials tamper radically with it. The Roman authorities rejected this altered Rule, and now Alphonsus and his Neapolitans were excluded from the congregation which he had founded.

In early life, Alphonsus had made a vow not to waste a moment of time; and he was faithful to death which came for him at the age of 92.

If he was tough-minded in pursuing the one thing necessary, Alphonsus was at all times a man of tender heart. I think of him taking off his shoes not to disturb his brethren at siesta time, and of his vehement insistence on the care of the sick—even the precious books were to be sold rather than anyone suffer neglect. When bishop, he stripped the house to make money to feed the poor. To the consternation of the officials he tried to get his hand on the cathedral treasures for the same purpose.

He was astonishingly forgiving. Nothing so threatened his congregation—so vulnerable at law—than court cases. For twenty years he was plagued by them due to a certain Maffei. Yet when Maffei died, Alphonsus immediately took over all his debts and saw to the education of his family. A letter survives from one of Maffei's sons thanking Alphonsus for taking the place of their "dear father" in his care for them. When Fr Mazzini, conscious of the harm he had done at Naples, feared to return to his community, Alphonsus, broken-hearted though he was, urged him warmly to return, saying that he himself was to blame.

In modern times the great Italian, Benedetto Croce, himself a Neapolitan, shows an instinctive understanding of the personality of Alphonsus. For him Alphonsus was a true representative of the Gospel spirit of moderation and clemency. He was indeed, in an age of rigorism, a preacher of God's mercy and of hope. He could say at the end of a

long life in pastoral ministry that he had never sent away a
penitent without absolution, and had never barred the
approach to communion.

His sensitivity of feeling, shown to people, had an outlet
also in artistic gifts, which he used for the glory of God. In
the British Museum is preserved a musical composition by
the saint, a cantata rated highly by the critics. Among the
many popular hymns which he composed is the best-known
Italian Christmas carol: "Tu scendi dalle stelle."

Alphonsus had an extremely delicate conscience; easy on
others, he was severe on himself. The tendency to scruples
he inherited from his mother, and from rigid moral attitudes
of the time, which he was to do much to change. His diary
reveals the painstaking efforts he made to discern truth in
action. There is, for instance, the letter he wrote in his old
age to his brother about the sale of two horses:

> I do not want to have any scruple about the horses
> I'm sending you. You will therefore let intending
> buyers know that one of them suffers in its jaws and
> cannot chew either straw or oats, and that the other,
> the older of the two, suffers from lunacy, and
> throws himself on the ground from time to time. To
> make him get up you must pull his ears. Explain all
> this clearly so that I may be at ease.

In the light of this, we may appreciate all the more the
cost to Alphonsus of his greatest written work, the *Moral
Theology*, which he edited many times in his own lifetime.
Through the book he cleared moral teaching from extreme
views, weighing up the evidence with a sure touch. Truth
always comes first with him; when it is clear, the opinions
of theologians one way or the other do not count. When it
is not clear, he provides sound principles to weigh up
opinions. The French theologian, P. Labourdette, OP, sums
up the contribution Alphonsus made to moral theology:

He bequeathed a body of really sure moral opinions, as far removed from one extreme as from another, carefully weighed by the conscience of a saint. To have done this was to have rendered an outstanding service to the Church. He was a moral theologian of exceptional greatness.

The people's missioner

When a man gives himself entirely to God he becomes free to serve his fellow men; belonging to God, he belongs also to all God's people. Alphonsus was truly a sent man, a missionary. All the ardour and skill of his advocacy was devoted to sharing his experience of God's love with his fellow men. When he was ordained, the first field of his missionary zeal was Naples, and his special concern there were the down-and-outs, the lazzaroni. He was inventive in reaching them where they were, organising "evening chapels" for prayer and discussion in such places as barber shops. If he could not come himself, the barber would take over. After a few years, there were 300 such "evening chapels" meeting regularly in Naples.

But Naples had priests in plenty, and in his journey to Scala Alphonsus found the country and mountain folk very much neglected. To meet this need he established his congregation of missioners. Now his zeal had new scope and support; its great instrument was to be the parish mission which he organised and developed to become a means of thorough-going renewal of all Christian life. With his companions he threw himself into this work, with its great sermons, catechetical instructions, sacraments, and the dramatic ceremonies so dear to Neapolitans. What he felt about missions is clear from his words: "What a privilege to be called by God as Christ was called by the Father to bring the light of faith and the warmth of hope and love into the hearts of men. Certainly the missions are one of the most effective means of bringing this about."

What made St Alphonsus a writer was this same missionary energy. His books are simply a prolongation of the missions. Just as he wrote the *Moral Theology* to help his students prepare for hearing confessions on missions, so too he began to write popular works of devotion to counteract the blighting influence of Jansenism which he saw at work among the people. The titles of his books read like a list not only of mission themes but also of the devotional exercises that overcame Jansenism in the Church: *The Eternal Truths, Preparation for Death, Meditations on the Incarnation* and *Meditations on the Passion, Visits to the Blessed Sacrament* (so popular that it appeared in German within a few years), *The Glories of Mary* (decisive in its influence on Marian devotion), *Novena to the Holy Spirit* and *Novena to the Sacred Heart*. (He saw quickly the value of this new devotion and defended it against the writer who later became Benedict XIV.)

During his busy days as bishop, he found time to write books for his clergy on the Mass, the divine office and the psalms. At the same time, conscious of his responsibilities towards the whole Church, he wrote a series of books in defence of the faith. All this writing was for the glory of God, so he refused to take profits from the publisher Remondini of Venice. In all, he wrote 110 works, big and small. That he met a need in the Church is evident from the spread of his writings to every country and language. After the Bible, he is claimed to be the best-seller, 20,000 editions in all. Countless Catholics have expressed their love of God in his words. One old lady in the far Philippines expressed well his influence: "He warms my heart."

Of course, there is a timebound element in the writing of Alphonsus; he was a man of his time, meeting its special needs. Moreover, his ardent Neapolitan temperament put off such critics as Dollinger in Germany and Pusey in

England; although Newman wisely remarked that he wrote for Neapolitans "whom he knew and we do not". It must be remembered especially that Alphonsus was a people's man; no doctor of the Church has been so popular a writer both in the extent and depth of his influence. Contact with the poor and simple people helped him speak from heart to heart in a clear direct style—a marvel for his time. Pastoral practice was everything to him; he was a man of practice and life. This gives a quality of immediacy to him as a man and as a writer; but it involves a corresponding limitation in his approach to theology, which is psychological rather than speculative.

Given these limitations, his works contain enduring treasures of practical wisdom in a variety of areas of Christian living. This is especially true of his letters which, as with other saints, are the least timebound of his writings. An editor comments:

> There is nothing useless, nothing which does not go straight to the point; if he speaks of asceticism, there is no far-fetched theorising; if he disputes, he shows a marvellous self-control which reveals the man whose only preoccupation is to discover truth.

In his books Alphonsus quotes a great deal. When he presents the faith, for instance, what counts for him is not his own faith so much as the faith of all the Christian centuries. He has a strong Christian sense of the Spirit at work in the communion of the Church down the ages. His books, it has been well said, become a pulpit in which prophets, apostles, Fathers of the Church, come forward to bear witness, their words now caught up in the living faith of Alphonsus. When he deals with Christian life, the saints fill his pages because they are experts. Above all, what concerns Alphonsus as he writes is the vital truth that the very same grace and redeeming love which transformed the saints is now at work in himself and in his readers. What all need most is to open themselves here and now to this grace. To make this point, Alphonsus wrote; to make it he worked and suffered to the end.

His spirituality: a summary

He wanted everyone to be saved and to become a saint, because God wanted it. He encouraged his missioners in every sermon to have this desire at heart for their hearers and for the whole human race.

All holiness consists in loving God, the end and the means to it. It is easier to do more than to do less, to give oneself completely to God than to give oneself in pieces. Easy, but only with the realisation that God has planted the seed in our hearts. He never stops repeating that holiness lies in loving God and man with the infinite love that God through the sacrifice of Christ wills to pour abundantly into hearts; this divine love alone can satisfy our hearts. The law of love is less a command than a gift.

To love God is to unite ourselves to Christ, our redeemer and friend. Christ is the centre of Alphonsus' life and work, the devotion of all devotions. Christ reveals and gives the love of God in crib, cross and tabernacle. Of all his books the best perhaps is *The Practice of the Love of Jesus Christ*; it is autobiography in the sense that it is what Alphonsus is all about.

The fullness of holiness involves the practice of two things detachment, and union with God. Here he strips down the traditional three ways to an essential twofold rhythm. No one insists more on detachment; he is merciless on tepidity. But for him detachment is only the other side of attachment to the Lord.

Union with God means above all else union with his will, to the point of identification, wanting nothing but what he wants. "Let us ask not so much for a tender love as for a strong love."

Since love and perseverance in it are gifts, humble, persevering prayer is as essential as breathing is to life. Love and prayer are then the two poles of his spirituality. A third is confidence in the motherly intercession of Mary.

There is much to wonder at in the life of Alphonsus, for instance, his extraordinary capacity and tenacity in work, and his vast experience in every department of Christian life. To see him fully, one must hold together the contrasting elements in him: the ardour of a poet and the calm balanced judgment of a judge at law; massive research and a childlike devotion to the authority of the Church; the flame of mysticism and a dispassionate objectivity in weighing the sordid extremes of conduct; his life dedicated to the principle: "give yourself entirely to God" and at the same time, his defence of a system of morality whose leading principle is "a doubtful law does not bind".

His achievements have been underlined by nearly all the popes since his time. He renewed the spirit of Christian life and piety, playing a decisive role in overcoming Jansenism as a force in the Church. He prepared the way for the definitions of the immaculate conception, the primacy and infallibility of the pope. He is largely responsible for the acceptance of the teaching of Mary's universal intercession. His moral teaching is the doctrine of confidence in God, good and merciful Father, who gives to men the means necessary for living Christian life and thereby attaining salvation. He shows to spiritual guides a safe and secure path along which to walk without fear.

> In truth the saint, more than any other doctor of the Church, seems to belong to our time, by his

magnificent pastoral activities, by the forms of the apostolate he introduced, and especially by his excellent books which still today are read by the faithful to their great spiritual profit. In these writings the figure of the saint still seems to live and his voice to resound, that inspired voice which gently attracted all those who listened to it, inflaming them with burning love for God, and which teaches us how we ̣hould preach the word of God.

(Pope Paul)

Alphonsus and prayer

St Alphonsus is called the doctor of prayer, and as we turn his pages we see that his spirituality rests on prayer. Wherever we go with him, we go with prayer. He repeats over and over: "Pray, pray, never cease praying," but he does more, he shows us how to pray as if our life depended on it, for he knows it does. This is clear from the gospels. The Gospel way of being human is sheer gift; and the only way to receive the gift is to open our hearts by desire. Christian life, then, is lived by borrowing, i.e. by prayer. Once we begin to pray, God's kingdom begins to grow in us; and to the extent that we keep on praying, we become people ruled by love. What is most condemned in the Gospel is the pharisee attitude of spiritual self-sufficiency which takes our goodness for granted. To become aware that our goodness is granted, we must take part in the vital activity of asking for it.

The first sin, then, existentially is not to pray, not to be in God's hands. At the root of all prayer, for Alphonsus, is a general kind of petition that God be all, that our prayer be fully for him, that we may belong to him completely. This dependence on prayer led him to coin the phrase which sums up his teaching memorably: "He who prays will be saved; he who does not pray will be lost." In 1759 he published *Prayer, the great means of salvation* on this theme: "I do not think that I have written a more useful work than this. . . If it were in my power I would distribute a copy of it to every Catholic in the world."

All his skill in persuasion is used here to prove that

151

prayer is vital. At the time, the theologians were caught up in deep argument about the mystery of grace and predestination. Under Jansenist influence, some doubted God's will to save all men. Alphonsus passionately defends God's will and merciful providence. No one lacks the essential grace to pray, and if they pray, they will thereby receive all further graces of holiness they need. His teaching on grace is personal and practical. Man encounters God in prayer and out of this encounter his personal salvation must come.

With Alphonsus, however, prayer is not primarily a matter of ideas or of teaching; it is a way of life with a logic and psychology all its own. He is never satisfied just to talk about prayer or convince minds about it. Full truth is not just truth in the mind; it is lived truth, the flesh and blood truth of concrete living. Only he who does the truth really knows. This is true of prayer; in Dom Chapman's words: "The only way to learn prayer is by praying." For Alphonsus, prayer is flesh of his flesh, bone of his bone; it trembles in him as he writes, his words being in harmony with the whole throbbing movement of his desire for God. You cannot separate the words from the praying man who wrote them.

Some have been tempted to dismiss Alphonsus as a devout writer, not a scientific theologian, especially since he does not use the formal language of theology. Yet a solid theological framework underlies all his work. Moreover, we ought to be clear what we mean by theology. There is theology as an academic discipline, in which one can get a degree; but this is not the true theology. One could be a doctor of academic theology without being in love with God. True theology is that which is lived by a doctor of the Church, who is a theologian in the deepest sense. Such was Alphonsus. If he were writing these lines, he would have the reader afire with prayer. According to Kierkegaard, "a theologian is one who not only talks of God but talks to God". From his first words to the last, Alphonsus writes of God, from God, to God, for God's people. When not explicit prayer, what he writes comes from prayer and leads to prayer.

Here again, his aim is missionary, to draw the reader into the movement to God. He wants to set desire on foot, and to reach the will, "the master of the soul"; to this end he works on the heart. But obviously the whole process calls for a "lettore devoto"—a reader committed in some way to prayer. A "profane" reader cannot meet Alphonsus in depth; he sees only words, ideas, and will easily blame Alphonsus for his own shallowness. It is true to say that beauty is in the eyes of the beholder, and that deep answers deep. One reader may see in Shakespeare's *King Lear* a primitive story; another more perceptive may discover in it the heart of Shakespeare; another again may find here the whole tragedy of human life.

In Christian tradition, the full process of prayer is four-fold: Listening to the Word, or divine reading; Meditation or reflection; Prayer proper, the unfolding of the will in praise; Contemplation, cleaving to God in mind and heart. All these elements of prayer are treated by Alphonsus, but in his own way and presented with an art all his own, emphasising what is most practical and useful for life.

There is no subject to which he returns more often than prayer proper—affective prayer of love, thanks, appeal, sorrow. Prayer in this sense is absolutely necessary for salvation, especially prayer of petition, which in our earthly, pilgrim condition is the most typical form of our prayer. But for him petition is not a pious beggary for material needs (which we could meet by our own efforts). No, it is a sublime beggary for God himself. In his *Way of the cross* and *Visits to the Blessed Sacrament*, Alphonsus keeps asking for the essential gifts: the love of God, final perseverance, and the grace to pray (this is especially characteristic of him).

Arising from the absolute need of prayer proper is the

moral need of mental prayer. This is so because if we do not take time to reflect on the truths of faith and to make them personal convictions, we shall remain blind both to them and to our need to pray. He would have his missionaries encourage everyone to make mental prayer. Through it, he sees the human heart becoming a paradise, where we talk with God as with a dearest friend. It is more important than vocal prayer, too much of which tires the mind and hinders reflection.

What are we to pray about?

First, about the eternal truths—the eternal dimension of human life. The effect is to detach us from sin and keep us humble before God. But we ought to pass from, "what does it profit a man to gain the whole world?" to the positive attitude of, "it is good for me to cling to my God". The severity of Alphonsus is more apparent than real. In his day, imagination and nerves were more robust, and serious devotion was not frightened by the great truths. Besides, he always scatters among the austere truths comforting thoughts of God's mercy, of the Passion and of our Lady. He castigates preachers who inspire nothing but fear: "What is done solely through fear of punishment and not through love won't last long."

Secondly, about God's goodness—shown especially in the mysteries of our Lord's life. The Passion is the favourite theme of prayer: "In it better than in any book we see the evil of sin and the love of God."

A practical rule is: "above all, choose subjects in which you find the greatest devotion." He repeats often that the aim of mental prayer is to unite us to God by love and to his will by good action.

Method of prayer

His description of mental prayer embodies the whole of his method:

> It is nothing more than a dialogue between the person and God. We pour out affections, desires, fears, requests, and God speaks to the heart, causing us to know his goodness and love, and what to do to please him.

We begin by putting ourselves in God's presence by faith, with a humble request for help. Reflection or reading provides us with material for dialogue: "Pause when you feel moved."

For Alphonsus the benefit of mental prayer lies not in the meditation as such, but in the affections, petitions, resolutions, i.e. the activity of the will. Best of all are the acts of love in its many forms, because love "ones" us with God, which is the whole point of prayer. If we feel dry, a great refuge is a humble request for more love.

His whole approach is flexible: "If the Holy Spirit inspires you with a movement of love at the beginning, don't meditate but allow the movement full freedom." As taught by Alphonsus, prayer is above all affective. Reflection sets the heart alight; the heart is moved only to move the will, and so subject the entire person to God. There is no room for sentimentality here.

Contemplation

St Alphonsus put together for confessors an abridgment of mystical theology; but in his writings for the general public, he stresses that holiness is measured not by extraordinary graces, but by detachment from all things (including such mystic graces) in order to be conformed to God's will. This emphasis on holiness available to all through active union with God's will is obviously meant to counteract two extreme attitudes of his time: Jansenism which made man helpless before God; and Quietism, which inculcated a completely passive attitude at prayer.

But if Alphonsus understandably avoids the language of mysticism, he does convey the living experience of God's purifying action in prayer through another and safer emphasis, i.e. on spiritual aridity. No doubt his own experience is at work here: the infirmities, scruples, internal and external torments of his life. Through such hammer blows God shapes us for heaven; shining through the darkness of aridity is the flame of God's love.

The Vatican Council has restored in our day the original sense of contemplation, which is a cleaving to God in mind and heart; in doing so it has left behind the complicated, often rarefied, elite notion of the past few centuries. This is where Alphonsus' approach to prayer becomes relevant to our time. For him too the heart of prayer is cleaving to God in will. In the expression "cleaving to God in mind and heart", what was meant traditionally was cleaving to him in my deepest self, in my spirit. The mind (*mens*) is not the thinking intelligence but the spirit, what we would call the "will". Certainly, we need discipline of mind for prayer, but as a means to help the clinging of the will to God. Good prayer is loving prayer and nothing else ultimately. The whole effort of Alphonsus is to move us to this self-surrender in living faith to God which is contemplative prayer. The intense petition for divine love repeated over and over in his writings is simply a way of expressing contemplative surrender to God. In his booklet: *How to converse continually and familiarly with God*, the contemplative unity of all prayer is brought out in simple everyday terms. In the old days, this book was to be found in many homes, a source of inner joy and serenity, making God's presence in the midst of life vividly real to its readers.

There is no end of writing on Christian spirituality today,

with plenty to remind us of what we ought to become if we are to embody the good news of Christ. In the midst of all this reading material when we begin to ask: "How am I to become what I want to be?", it's good to turn to Alphonsus. His message is not new, but it is very down to earth, startlingly clear and relentless in demand: "Begin now to be what you say you are. Pray, pray, open out your deep heart in desire. If you want it hard enough, the gift will come. If you want God hard enough, you will be possessed by him."

Gerald Crotty, CSsR

Notes

1 St Augustine: his life, times and spirituality

1. London 1973.
2. Quoted in the *Ampleforth Journal* 29 (Spring 1975) 1.
3. Cf. C. BOYER S J , "Saint Augustine" in the *Month* (August 1959), p. 74.
4. M. O'C. DARCY, *The Danger of Words*, (London 1973), p. 31.
5. E. GILSON, *The Christian Philosophy of Saint Augustine*, Trans. by L. E. M. Lynch (London, 1961), p. ix.
6. For the text of Celestine's letter see E. PORTALIE S.J., *A Guide to the Thought of Saint Augustine*, Trans. by R. J. Bastian SJ (London 1960), p. 316.
7. Cf. *De beata vita*, 35: PL 32, 976.
8. *Sermo 293*, 7: PL 38, 1332. Cf. *Sermo 26*, 6, 7: PL 38, 173-4.
9. "Deus enim deum te vult facere: non natura sicut est ille quem genuit; sed dono suo et adoptione." *Sermo 166*, 4: PL 38, 909.
10. There is a vital distinction between self-love and selfishness, as will be seen later.
11. *In Joannis evangelium*, tract. 26, 2: PL 35, 1607.
12. "Signum eius est humilitas eius." *In Joannis evangelium*, tract 3: PL 35, 1396.
13. *Sermo 69*, 1, 2: PL 38, 441. Cf. *Enarratio in psalmum 119*: PL 37, 1596. F. VAN DER MEER, *Augustine the bishop*, trs. B. Battershaw and G. R. Lamb, (London 1961), p. xxi, says Augustine practised the virtue of humility to a "heroic degree".
14. *The Art of Loving* (London 1957), p. 133.
15. *Soliloquia*, I, 1, 1: PL 32, 885.
16. Cf. *Enarratio in psalmum 41*, 13: PL 36, 473. See also *Confessiones* IV, 14, 22: PL 32, 702.
17. *Sermo 121*, 1: PL 38, 678. Cf. *De moribus ecclesiae catholicae*, I, 1: PL 32, 1319.
18. Commenting on the first epistle of St John, 4:20, Augustine

declares that the reason why one does not love God is because one does not see him, and the reason one does not see him is because one does not love. Cf. *In epistolam Joannis ad Parthos*, tract 9, 10: PL 35, 2052. Cf. also *De trinitate*, VIII, 8, 1: PL 42, 958-60.

19. *Enarratio in psalmum 118, Sermo 8*, 2: PL 37, 1520. I have slightly altered Augustine's text in translation. Cf. also *De trinitate*, VIII, 4, 6: PL 42, 951.

20. Cf. *De moribus ecclesiae*, I, 25, 47: PL 32, 1331. In this connection one will recall Augustine's expressions, *ad veritatem per charitatem* and *charitas novit eam* (the truth).

21. *Confessiones*, III, 1, 1: PL 32, 683. I have used Frank Sheed's brilliant translation which admirably succeeds in reproducing the flavour of Augustine's idiom. Cf. *The Confessions of St Augustine* (Sheed & Ward, London 1943), p. 39.

22. *Confessiones*, 8-9, 13-14: PL 32, 699; Sheed, op. cit. pp. 65-66.

23. Quoted from an article by T. J. VAN BAVEL OSA, "The evangelical inspiration of the rule of St Augustine", in the *Downside Review* 93 (1975) 92.

24. *Enarratio in psalmum 31*, 2, 5: PL 36, 260.

25. E. FROMM, op. cit., p. 132.

26. Cf. *In epistolam Joannis ad Parthos*, tract. 10, 10: PL 35, 2052.

27. We could not love, says Augustine, unless God first loved us. Cf. *In epistolam Joannis ad Parthos*, tract. 9, 9: PL 35, 2051.

28. Cf. *De civitate dei*, XIV, 30, 8: PL 41, 436. Cf. *De genesi ad litteram*, XI, 15: PL 34, 437.

29. 'Magis enim inhumanum, non amare in homine quod homo est, sed amare quod filius est: hoc est enim non in eo amare illud quod ad Deum pertinet, sed amare illud quod ad se pertinet." (*De vera religione*, 46, 88: PL 34, 161).

30. E. FROMM, op. cit., pp. 58, 60, makes this point very well.

31. *Enarratio in psalmum 31*, 2, 5: PL 36, 260.

32. *Confessiones*, X, 29, 40; 31, 45; 37, 60: PL 32, 796, 798, 804. Cf. *De spiritu et littera*, 13, 22: PL 44, 214.

33. Cf. *Enchiridion*, 32: PL 40, 248.

34. *Sermo 108*, 5: PL 38, 634.

35. Cf. *In epistolam Joannis ad Parthos*, tract. 2, 11: PL 35, 1995.

36. Ibid., 14: PL 35, 1997.

37. Cf. *Sermo 344*, 2: PL 38, 1512.

38. *Sermo 34*, 4, 4: PL 38, 212.

39. *De moribus ecclesiae*, I, 36, 48: PL 32, 1331. Cf. *In Joannis evangelium*, tracts 83, 3; 87, 1: PL 35, 1846, 1852.

40. Cf. *Sermo 265*, 8, 9: PL 38, 1223.

41. Cf. *In epistolam Joannis ad Parthos*, tract. 10, 3: PL 35, 2056.

42. *De moribus ecclesiae*, I, 33, 73: PL 32, 1341. Cf. *In Joannis evangelium*, tract. 9, 8: PL 35, 1462.

43. *In Joannis evangelium*, tract. 83, 3: PL 35, 1846.

44. Op. cit., p. 47.

45. Cf. *De moribus ecclesiae*, I, 25, 46: PL 32, 1331.

46. *Sermo 265*, 8, 9: PL 38, 1222.

47. Cf. *De trinitate*, VIII, 8, 12: PL 42, 958.

48. Ibid., 7, 10: PL 42:956.

49. Cf. *De trinitate*, VIII, 8, 12: PL 42, 959; *Epistola 130*, 7, 14: PL 33, 499.

50. *In epistolam Joannis ad Parthos*, tract. 7, 8: PL 35, 2033. Cf. *Expositio epistolae ad Galatas*, 57: PL 35, 2144.

51. *In epistolam Joannis ad Parthos*, loc. cit.

52. *St Augustine and his influence through the ages*, trs. P. Hepburne-Scott (London 1957), p. 80.

Augustine and Prayer

1. Cf. J. MOISER, "When you pray. . .the prayer of petition" in *The Way* 16 (1976) 75. It would be wrong to dismiss the article as an idiosyncratic analysis of the prayer of petition, however one may feel obliged to dissent from the author's viewpoint.

2. Augustine, as we shall see, did write an exceptionally long letter in answer to a request concerning petitionary prayer, but his reply, which indeed goes beyond its immediate object, cannot be regarded as a treatise on prayer.

3. In the circumstances one cannot be warmly commend the study by THOMAS A. HAND, OSA, *St Augustine on Prayer* (Dublin 1963).

4. "Ipsum enim desiderium tuum, oratio tua est" (*Enarratio in psalmum 37*, 1: PL 36, 404). On prayer as desire cf. CH. A. BERNARD, SJ, "La Prière chrétienne—étude théologique: *Essai pour notre temps* 3 (Bruges-Paris 1967), pp. 49-51 and *passim*.

5. *Sermo 168*, 5: PL 38: 913-4.

6. *Epistola 194*, 3, 10: PL 33, 878. Cf. *Enchiridion*, 7, 2: PL 40, 234.

7. "Magnae vires et cursus celerrimus praeter viam." (*Enarratio in psalmum 31*, 2, 4: PL 37, 259). Cf. *Sermo 141*, 4, 4: PL 35, 377); *In epistolam Joannis ad Parthos*, tract. 10, 1: PL 35, 2054.

8. *Enarratio in psalmum 103*, 1, 19: PL 37, 1352.

9. Cf. *Epistola 194*, 4, 16: PL 33, 879-880.

10. *De vera religione*, 39, 72: PL 34, 154.

11. *Soliloquia*, I, 1, 1: PL 32, 885.

12. *Confessiones*, III, 6, 10-11: PL 32, 687-8. Here as elsewhere I have used the translation by Frank Sheed, *The Confessions of St Augustine* (Sheed & Ward, London 1943), pp. 45-7.

13. *Soliloquia*, II, 6, 9: PL 32, 889.

14. Cf. *In Joannis evangelium*, tract. 18, 10: PL 35, 1541-2.

15. *Epistola 120*, 1, 5: PL 33, 454.

16. *Confessiones*, X, 40, 65: PL 32, 807; Sheed, op. cit., p. 189.

17. *Confessiones*, IX, 10, 24: PL 32, 774.

18. *De sermone domini in monte*, II, 3, 14: PL 34, 1275.

19. Cf. *Confessiones*, X, 6, 8: PL 32, 782-3.

20. *Sermo 91*, 3, 3: PL 38, 568. Cf. *Enarratio in psalmum 137*, 2: PL 37, 1775; *Epistola 140*, 17, 44: PL 33, 557.

21. *In epistolam Joannis ad Parthos*, tract. 4, 6: PL 35, 2008.

22. Cf. *De dono perseverantiae*, 23, 63-5: PL 45, 1031-3.

23. *Epistola 130*, 9, 18: PL 33, 501.

24. *Sermo 56*, 4, 4: PL 38, 379.

25. What Augustine actually wrote is that it is neither wrong nor useless to pray at length: "Cum diu orare vacat. . . non est improbum nec inutile." (*Epistola 130*, 10, 19: PL 33, 501).

26. Cf. *Epistola 130*, 10, 20: PL 33, 501.

27. Cf. *Epistola 130*, 15, 28: PL 33, 505.

28. Cf. *Enarratio in psalmum 139*, 15: PL 37, 1812.

29. Cf. Gregory the Great: "Oratione operatio, et operatione fulciatu oratio." (*Moralia*, 18, 5, 10: PL 76, 42-43).

30. *Epistola 48*, 1: PL 33, 188.

31. *De opere monachorum*, 29, 37: PL 40, 576.

32. Cf. *Epistola 48*, 2: PL 33, 188; *De civitate dei*, XIX, 19: PL 41, 647.

33. *Epistola 130*, 9, 18: PL 33, 501.

34. *Vita s. Aurelii Augustini*, 24: PL 32, 54.

35. F. VAN DER MEER, *Augustine the Bishop*, trs. B. Battershaw and G. R. Lamb (London 1961), p. 305, says Augustine created the language of western piety.

36. *Epistola 130*, 4, 9: PL 33, 497. Cf. columns 494-507 for the full text of the letter.

37. *Epistola 130*, 8, 15: PL 33, 499.

38. Cf. *Epistola 130*, 14, 27: PL 33, 505.

39. Cf. H. DENZINGER, *Enchiridion symbolorum*, 30th edition, ed. K. Rahner, SJ (Freiburg im Breisgau 1955, no. 804). Cf. AUGUSTINE, *De natura et gratia*, 43, 50: PL 44, 271. Cf. also *De dono perseverantiae*, 5, 10: PL 45, 999; *De gratia et libero arbitrio*, 15: PL 44, 890-1.

40. Cf. *Epistola 130*, 12, 22,23: PL 33, 502-3; *De sermone domini in monte*, II, 4, 15: PL 35, 1275; *Enarratio in psalmum 103*, 1, 19: PL 37, 1352.

41. Cf. *De sermone domini in monte*, II, 7, 26: PL 35, 1280.

42. Cf. *De sermone domini in monte*, II, 4, 15—11, 39: PL 34, 1275-1287.

43. *De magistro*, 1, 2: PL 32, 1195.

44. Cf. HAND, op. cit., pp. 95-117.

45. On the distinction between social love and private love see especially AUGUSTINE, *De genesi ad litteram*, XI, 15, 20: PL 34, 437.

46. *Enarratio in psalmum 85*, 1: PL 37, 1081-2. Cf. *Sermo 57*, 2, 2: PL 38, 387. See also the *General Instruction on the Liturgy of the Hours*, no. 7.

47. Cf. *Sermo 61*, 5, 6: PL 38, 411; *Epistola 130*, 8, 17: PL 33, 500.

48. Cf. *Epistola 130*, 8, 17: PL 33, 501.

49. Cf. *Confessiones*, X, 35, 57: PL 32, 803, Other references to distractions will be found in *Enarratio in psalmum 140*, 18: PL 37, 1827-8; *Sermo 56*, 8-9, 12: PL 38, 382-3.

50. Cf. *Enarratio in psalmum 103*, 1, 4: PL 37, 1338; *Epistola 140*, 14, 36: PL 33, 554.

51. Cf. *Confessiones*, IX, 4, 8-12: PL 32, 766-9.

52. *Regula* (Praeceptum), 1, 2, ed. LUC VERHEIJEN, OSA, *La règle de saint Augustin*, i (Paris 1967), 417.

53. Cf. *Sermo 267*, 4, 4: PL 38, 1231.

54. *In epistolam Joannis ad Parthos*, tract. 6, 10: PL 35, 2025. Cf. *De civitate dei*, XVIII, 49: PL 41, 162; *Enarratio in psalmum 130*, 5: PL 37, 1706; *Sermo 265*, 10, 12: PL 38, 1224; *Sermo 267*, 3, 3: PL 38, 1230.

55. Cf. *In epistolam Joannis ad Parthos, loc. cit.*

56. *In epistolam Joannis ad Parthos*, tract. 6, 10: PL 35, 2025-6.

57. Cf. *In epistolam Joannis ad Parthos*, tract. 6, 13: PL 35, 2028.

58. Cf. *Epistola 55*, 18, 34: PL 33, 221.

59. *In epistolam Joannis ad Parthos*, tract. 6, 10: PL 35, 2025.

2 St Bernard: his life, times and spirituality

1. *Apologia* IX, 19; S. *Bernardi Opera* Vol. III, *Tractatus et Opuscula*; critical edition by J. Leclercq OSB and H. M. Rochais; Rome: Editiones Cistercienses 1963.

2. On Saint Bernard in history, see David Knowles, *The Christian Centuries*, Vol. Two, *The Middle Ages* London 1969.

3. Circumcision Sermon 3, 10; S.*Bernardi Opera* Vol. IV, *Sermones* 1; critical edition by J. Leclercq, OSB, and H. Rochais; Rome: Editiones Cistercienses 1966.

4. Letter 76 (73, 1, in Latin) in *The Letters of St Bernard*. Translated by Bruno Scott James; London, Burns Oates 1953.

5. Letter 77.

6. Letter 73.

7. This summary is based on that of Arnold of Bonnevaux, *Vita Prima* Book 2, chapter 6, 40.

8. Canticle Sermon 83, 5. Quotations from Canticle Sermons from the late Fr Ailbe Luddy's *St Bernard's Sermons on the Canticle*, two volumes; Browne and Nolan, Dublin, 1920; slight changes have been made.

9. *Ibid*. 49, 5 and ff.

10. *Ibid.* 50, 5 and ff.

11. *Ibid*. 57, 9.

Bernard and prayer

1. *Romans* 8, 16: Dedication of Church Sermon 5, 7; All Saints Sermon 2, 3; S. *Bernardi Opera* Vol. V, *Sermones* II; critical edition by J. Leclercq OSB, and H. Rochais; Rome, Editiones Cistercienses 1968.

2. *Sententiae* Series 1, 2; S. *Bernardi Opera*, Vol. VI, 2, *Sermones* III; critical edition by J. Leclercq OSB and H. Rochais; Rome: Editiones Cistercienses 1972.

3. Christmas Eve Sermon 2, 7.

4. "On How God Should Be Loved; De Diligendo Deo"; S. *Bernardi Opera* Vol. III.

5. Saint John the Baptist Sermon 1.

6. "In Praise of the Virgin Mother: In Laudibus Virginis Matris", (four homilies on *Luke* 1:26-38), 4, 11; S.*Bernardi Opera* Vol. IV.

7. *Sermones De Diversis*; S. *Bernardi Opera* Vol. VI, 1; critical edition Leclercq-Rochais; Rome: Editiones Cistercienses 1970.

8. On Conversion IV, 6.
9. *Diversis* Sermon 29, 2; Canticle Sermons: 20, 4 and 6; 35, 6.
10. Pentecost Sermon 2, 3.
11. Sunday within Assumption Octave Sermon 1.
12. Advent Sermon 1, 1.
13. *Diversis* Sermon 25, 3; *Diversis* Sermon 107, 1; the latter echoes *Romans* 10:9-10.
14. Lent Sermon 5, 5 and 7.
15. *Canticle* Sermon 36, 5-6.
16. *Diversis* Sermon 25, 8.
17. *Timothy* 2:1: *Diversis* Sermons 25, 1; 107, 1.
18. All Saints Sermons 18, 6; 31, 5; 49, 4, etc.
19. *Canticle* Sermons 18, 6; 31, 5; 49, 4, etc.
20. On *Psalm 90* Sermon 10, 1; Letter 34, 1.
21. *Canticle* Sermon 21, 4-7.

4. Teresa and prayer

1. The late Father James Brodrick, SJ, says that this work by Ludolph of Saxony was the first formal Life of Christ ever written and, on the invention of printing, it was translated into the main European languages.

Contributors

Fr Michael Hackett, O.S.A., Ph. D., Austin Friars School, Scotland: master of novices, English vice-province, 1960-66; Vice-Provincial, 1966-73. He has written extensively on the spirituality of St Augustine.

Fr Hugh McCaffery, O.S.C.O., Mount Melleray Abbey: ordained in 1945; novice master, Mount Melleray, 1948-1957; an expert on the writings of St Bernard.

Fr Simon Tugwell, O.P., M.A., Blackfriars, Oxford: retreat master, broadcaster and preacher; has conducted many seminars on prayer; author of *Did you receive the Spirit?* and *Prayer*.

Miss Mary Purcell is author of *The Halo and the Sword, Dom Francisco, Matt Talbot and his Times, The First Jesuit, St Anthony and his Times, The Great Captain, The World of Monsieur Vincent*, and several other books and many articles.

Fr Richard McCullen, C.M., Provincial of the Vincentian Fathers; formerly spiritual director in Maynooth College.

Fr Gerald Crotty, C.Ss.R., D.D., Marianella Pastoral Centre: formerly professor of dogmatic theology.